HISTORIC SCOTLAND

SCOTTISH CATHEDRALS

SCOTTISH CATHEDRALS

RICHARD FAWCETT

B. T. Batsford Ltd / Historic Scotland

Typeset by Bernard Cavender Design & Greenwood Graphics Publishing
and printed by The Bath Press, Bath

Published by B. T. Batsford Ltd
583 Fulham Road, London SW6 5BY

A CIP catalogue record for this book is
available from the British Library

ISBN 0 7134 8188 9

(*Front cover*) Dunkeld Cathedral, the tower and nave

Contents

Illustrations

Colour plates

Foreword

Dr Richard Fawcett is well known throughout Scotland and far beyond its borders as an immensely knowledgeable, perceptive and sympathetic interpreter of the architecture and buildings of our past, especially of the medieval and early modern period. In *Scottish Abbeys and Priories* (1994) he gave a rich insight into the ways in which medieval religious orders sought architectural expression for their faith and their rule of communal life under strict discipline. Now, in *Scottish Cathedrals*, he demonstrates clearly, in a text which is easy to follow and with an abundance of well-chosen illustrations, the wealth, which for many still comes as a surprise, of Scotland's heritage of cathedral churches. For good measure, he takes the story right through to modern times, showing how cathedrals have certainly not been removed from the scene by the Reformation, the religious strife of the seventeenth century or the period of comparatively peaceful ecclesiastical co-existence in which we still live today.

Traditionally, the Scots have had an uneasy relationship with bishops – not for nothing is the plant which the English call 'ground elder' known in Scotland as 'bishop weed'. Yet some of the greatest figures of our past have been bishops: the patriots William Wishart, David Murray and William Lamberton, the educators William Turnbull, James Kennedy and William Elphinstone, and the statesmen and men of affairs David Bernham, Bernard of Arbroath, William Scheves and even David Beaton. Saints and sinners, the bishops have made an incalculable contribution to our history. Their chief churches, whose construction they inspired and commissioned, in which they must often have preached, and over the life of whose communities they presided, hold an abiding fascination. But cathedrals were not merely chief churches for bishops. For many centuries they stood as by far the most conspicuous symbol of the Christian faith for a largely illiterate people. In many parts of the country they would have been the only churches where worship by the laity would have had a musical setting. For all these reasons we should be keen to visit the cathedrals of Scotland, most of which, for obvious reasons, are easily accessible. Armed with Dr Fawcett's comfortably portable book, we shall understand how they came to be built, why they possess the architectural features that we can still see, how much may have been lost by destruction or neglect and where we can most sensibly look for other buildings which may have inspired or been inspired by the churches which the author describes so skilfully.

Geoffrey Barrow
Professor Emeritus of Scottish History,
University of Edinburgh

Preface and acknowledgements

Scotland's cathedrals are among our most rewarding architectural assets. Yet, although in recent years there has been a heartening increase in scholarly interest in them within the British Isles and Europe, and even from as far afield as North America, they still take many visitors by surprise. This book is aimed mainly at those general readers who have encountered our cathedrals and would like to understand a little more fully their architecture and the way they served the Church, as well as at those who are planning to visit them and wish to prepare themselves in advance.

A cathedral is the principal church of a bishop within his diocese, the area over which he exercised his spiritual authority. Scotland had some bishops from as early as the fifth century, but the oldest of our surviving cathedrals were started around the time of the major reorganization of the Church which took place in the late eleventh and twelfth centuries, and it was the thirteenth century that was to see the highest sustained levels of building activity. The years of warfare with England in the earlier part of the fourteenth century resulted in greatly reduced amounts of construction, but major works were again under way by the end of the fourteenth century at several of the cathedrals, and there are records of major building operations up to the eve of the Reformation. There are thus few parts of the Middle Ages from the twelfth century onwards which did not produce important cathedral work, and the

cathedrals continued to provide a testing-ground for new architectural thought throughout the period.

This changed after the Reformation in 1560. One reason for this was that the bishops were viewed with disfavour by the more radical reformers, until they were finally removed from the national Church in 1689, existing thereafter only in the splinter group which developed into the Episcopal Church, and later in the Catholic Church after the restoration of its hierarchy. But, quite apart from changed attitudes to bishops, the forms of worship introduced after the Reformation simply did not require complex church buildings. In view of the clear unsuitability of the cathedrals for such worship, we should perhaps be especially grateful to the reformed Church of Scotland that so many of them survived as well as they did until the revival of interest in medieval architecture which emerged from the later eighteenth century onwards. In the course of the nineteenth century, several cathedrals were to be restored to much of their former glory, while around the same period both the Episcopal and Roman Catholic Churches were granted greater freedom to worship, and eventually provided themselves with new cathedrals.

As a result of this complex history, Scotland now has twenty-seven churches in use that can be described as cathedrals. This book is mainly concerned with the thirteen churches that were built as cathedrals in the Middle Ages, five of which are no longer in use. However, for the sake of completeness, it was felt that some mention should also be made of the more recent cathedrals, and these are covered briefly in both the final chapter and the gazetteer. At the beginning of the gazetteer (p. 111) will be found a map showing the positions of all the cathedrals and cathedral sites referred to in the text, and the gazetteer should also be referred to for the plans of the cathedrals of medieval construction (see **76–90**).

I have built up debts of gratitude to a number of people in the preparation of this book. For reading through the draft and offering their comments I owe particular thanks to Professor Geoffrey Barrow (to whom I owe added thanks for the Foreword), to Professor Michael Lynch, Professor Donald Watt and, as always, to my wife, Sue. For help with information on a number of the more modern cathedrals I am grateful to Morag Cross and Dimitrios Theodouopoulis. The plans and map are the work of Kevin Hicks. The photographic work was carried out by Historic Scotland's photographers, for which I offer thanks to David Henrie and Chris Hutcheson.

Unless otherwise stated in the captions, all illustrations are copyright Historic Scotland.

1
The earliest cathedrals

Bishops and cathedrals in the early Church

The word 'cathedral' comes from the Latin *cathedra*, meaning a ceremonial chair or throne, and it was used to refer to the church within which a bishop placed his throne as the symbol of his authority in the area over which he exercised ecclesiastical control, which was itself known as a diocese. A cathedral did not necessarily have to be a large church, but it would always be a more effective symbol of authority if it were larger than most other churches within a diocese and, as cathedrals came to be the focus of an increasing number of functions, there was much to be said for them being big enough to house all of those functions comfortably. Since Christianity first developed within the context of the strongly urban Roman world, the earliest bishops generally had their main church within the principal city of the area under their pastorate, and the boundaries of their dioceses would usually conform with those of the administrative areas of the part of the empire in which they were situated.

The title 'bishop' is itself derived from the Greek *episcopos*, meaning an overseer. We know that there were bishops in the Church from a very early period as they are referred to in the New Testament, although it may not have been until a century or more had passed that they came to be considered as superior to ordinary priests. Nevertheless, they regarded themselves as the direct successors of the apostles in an unbroken chain involving the

laying on of hands from one generation to the next. In the western Church the bishops' dioceses were usually grouped into provinces, reflecting the similar division of the Roman empire into provinces, and eventually the chief bishop of each province came to be referred to as an archbishop, with metropolitan authority over the other bishops. These archbishops tended to act as the chief links with the Bishop of Rome who, since he regarded himself as the direct successor of St Peter, in the course of the Middle Ages increasingly successfully pressed his claim to be acknowledged as over-all head of much of the Church. Significantly, from the sixth century onwards the Bishop of Rome came to have almost exclusive use of the affectionately respectful title of papa or pope, a title previously used more generally by other senior clergy, even though it may not have been until the eleventh century that his claims to be head of the western Church gained general acceptance.

There were many ecclesiastical functions that only those of the rank of bishop could perform (1). These included the consecration of other bishops, the ordination of priests, the confirmation of baptized members of the Church, the dedication of church buildings, and the supervision of doctrinal orthodoxy. But bishops and senior clergy also tended to have high responsibilities in the secular world thrust upon them. Once Christianity had become the official religion of the Roman empire in the early

1 A medieval bishop wearing his mass vestments, and with his mitre on his head. Bishop Winchester of Elgin (1435–60) from his tomb in the cathedral.

fourth century, it was natural that its highest officials – who were increasingly from the patrician classes – should be drawn into affairs of state as well as being responsible for the government of the Church. This was even more the case after the collapse of the western empire, and the subsequent progressive re-establishment of a new form of order from the later eighth century, when the clergy were again of particular importance as being among the few fully literate members of society. As a result, there was a continuing demand for the services of bishops by national or local rulers, so that up to the end of the Middle Ages many of the higher clergy were also great officers of state. Indeed the grant of a bishopric might be a monarch's way of rewarding a valued priest in his service – it could even be the way in which that priest received such payment as he might expect. In this there were the seeds of conflict between secular rulers and the pope, since the latter was increasingly claiming the right to appoint all prelates of the Church. It might be added that the bishops and senior clergy were also tending to become great landowners, with all the administrative burdens that entailed, as they were granted estates to support their elevated status.

The first Scottish bishops

The first recorded person within what is now Scotland who is likely to have been a bishop is St Ninian, who probably served the Church in fifth-century Galloway, though he is also said by the Venerable Bede to have converted the southern Picts in the parts of Scotland north of the Forth. According to Bede he had been trained in Rome and, after returning to Galloway, built a church of stone known as Candida Casa (the white house – presumably because it was plastered or painted white), which was dedicated to St Martin of Tours. Ninian's cathedral is thought to have been at Whithorn, where there was later an Anglian monastery and then later still a medieval cathedral. (For a map of the cathedrals and cathedral sites referred to in the text see 75.) Excavation at the eastern end of the cathedral has revealed traces of a small rectangular plastered building which has been interpreted by some as Ninian's own cathedral, though there can be no certainty on this. More likely to date from nearer to Ninian's time are a number of inscribed or carved stones, one of which commemorates a man called Latinus and his daughter, which could be of the mid-fifth century.

According to later legend St Ninian also dedicated a graveyard at what is now Glasgow, within which St Kentigern (known also as Mungo) is said to have built a cathedral for his own diocese in the later sixth century. Kentigern, who died in 612, is thought to have been bishop of an area roughly corresponding with the British kingdom of Strathclyde. Puzzlingly, however, no real evidence has been found for ecclesiastical use of this site before the twelfth century, though this certainly does not rule out the possibility that Kentigern was bishop here. He is said also to have been based for a while at Hoddom in Dumfries-shire, and it may be that he had a cathedral church there as well. As at Whithorn, there was subsequently an Anglian monastery at Hoddom, and in both cases recent excavations have located important evidence for those monasteries.

There were bishops in other parts of Scotland in the following centuries, though there cannot have been anything approaching a systematic subdivision of the country into dioceses, as there was to be later. In any case, from the mid-sixth century onwards monasteries were for a while to assume greater importance than cathedrals as administrative centres for the Church. This was at least partly because the greatest impetus to Christian expansion in Scotland was to come from the west, with the colonization by the Scots from Ireland of those parts of the western seaboard known as Dalriada. The greatest landmark in this process was the foundation of the monastery of Iona by St Columba, or Colum Cille, in 563 or 565, which itself became the chief house of a *paruchia* (grouping) of partly interdependent monasteries. In this connection it should be remembered that Ireland was far less urbanized than continental Europe and, though its Church saw itself as an integral part of wider Christendom, a system of ecclesiastical control by bishops ruling territorial dioceses did not take root so readily there. Bishops were certainly needed within the Church for all the functions they alone could exercise, but it was the great monasteries founded by the ruling dynasties, and with members of those dynasties as their heads, that tended to dominate the Church. Sometimes bishops were members of those communities, possibly on occasion acting as both bishop and abbot; at Iona, for example, the fourth abbot, named as Fergna, who had been a companion of St Columba, is sometimes said to have been a bishop. However, this is doubtful and it is not until the eighth, ninth and tenth centuries that we can be more certain about the presence of bishops there. Elsewhere

in the late sixth and early seventh centuries it is possible that St Blane, a native of Bute who had been trained in Ireland, served as a bishop in the monastery at Kingarth on Bute, and possibly – though more contentiously – also at Dunblane.

Records of the existence of bishops become a little more frequent from the late seventh century, and especially in the Lowland areas where there was less influence from Ireland. In the course of the expansion of the Northumbrian Anglians into south-eastern Scotland their Bishop Trumwine briefly based his diocese on a monastery at Abercorn in West Lothian in the 680s, until he deemed it expedient to return to Northumbria after the defeat of the Anglians by the Pictish King Brude, son of Bile, at the battle of Nechtansmere in 685. Not long after that, however, the Pictish King Nechtan went on to seek the advice of the Northumbrians on a number of ecclesiastical matters in which it was felt their practices were closer to what was deemed acceptable within the wider European Church. A short-lived bishopric appears to have been established at Abernethy in Perthshire, possibly by King Nechtan himself, in the early eighth century, when there were a number of unnamed bishops.

In the following centuries there may have been bishops at a growing number of sites, including those where there were to be later cathedrals, and claims have been made for Brechin, Dunblane and Rosemarkie (the predecessor of Fortrose), though by far the most important episcopal centres to emerge around this period were to be at Dunkeld and Kinrimund (later known as St Andrews). As the Irish Scots extended their authority eastwards across Pictland, and with the added spur of the Norse raids down the west coast from the 790s onwards, in 849 King Kenneth macAlpin decided to remove the relics of St Columba from Iona. Some were taken to Dunkeld, which was at the very heart of his expanded kingdom, and it may have been that a bishopric with claims to authority over all others was established there at the same time. The chief evidence for this is that

Tuathal, abbot of the monastery of Dunkeld, was described at his death in 865 as being also the chief bishop of the kingdom, suggesting Dunkeld had become the Scottish ecclesiastical headquarters. This function, however, was soon to be taken over by Kinrimund on the Fife coast, where there had been a monastery since at least the eighth century or even, according to one improbable legend, from the fourth century. Relics thought to be of St Andrew – from which the place took its later name – could have reached there after Bishop Acca was exiled from his diocese of Hexham in 732, though the first reference to a religious community was on the death of one of its abbots in 747. But it is only from the start of the tenth century that there appears to have been a succession of bishops at Kinrimund who were evidently regarded as the most important in the kingdom, and who bore titles such as 'episcopus Scotorum' or 'epscop Alban' (bishop of the Scots or of Scotland).

More bishops come into the records in the course of the eleventh century in various parts of the country, including some in parts that were not yet under Scottish royal control. There were bishops for the Norse-controlled diocese of Orkney from possibly before 1035, for example, and for the diocese of the Isles, which was similarly under Norse control, from before 1079. The local rulers of the semi-independent province of Moray may also have appointed bishops by the later eleventh century. Other bishops are named from the mid-eleventh century for the diocese of Glasgow, although in that case it seems likely the earlier ones were little more than absentee assistants of the archbishops of York, who considered they had claims to metropolitan authority over the Scottish Church and were making use of the title of a vacant diocese. If any conclusion can be drawn from all of this, it is that by the eleventh century the Scottish Church had an established, if very unsystematic, tradition of being governed by bishops. But our knowledge of them at this time is still limited: we know little of the boundaries of their dioceses, and nothing of

churches that may have served as cathedrals.

This confusing picture was to become more focused from the early twelfth century, as the three sons of Malcolm III and St Margaret who ruled Scotland between 1097 and 1153 (Edgar, Alexander I and David I) brought their Church into the mainstream of a current of renewal sweeping across Christendom; in doing this they needed the help of bishops. At the kingdom's chief diocese at St Andrews, after two unsuccessful attempts to introduce suitable bishops, in 1124 Alexander I eventually arranged for the election of Robert, the head of the Augustinian priory of Scone. It was also in Alexander's reign, from the third decade of the century onwards, that a regular succession of bishops began to appear at Dunkeld.

As with so much that was achieved for the Church in the earlier twelfth century, the greatest contribution to the more systematic organization of the dioceses was probably made by David I, both before and after becoming king in 1124. As a younger son with little apparent prospect of succeeeding to the throne, he had spent much of his time since 1100 at the court of his brother-in-law, Henry I of England, where he was provided with the country's greatest heiress, Maud de Senlis, as his wife. As an intensely pious observer of the Church in both England and Europe, he was supremely well placed to be aware of all the ways in which the Church was being reformed and made more effective. He was also astute enough to appreciate that a systematically organized Church was a powerful additional tool in the hands of a ruler who wished to strengthen his own authority. At Glasgow, at a date between 1114 and 1118, he had the man who was earlier his tutor, John, introduced as bishop of those parts of Scottish Cumbria (later to be known as Strathclyde) over which his brother allowed him authority. To the south of Glasgow, Galloway was coming increasingly under royal control, and bishops were appointed there again from 1128, though for a variety of reasons the diocese was to remain within the province of the archbishops of York until the mid-fourteenth century. Elsewhere, bishops of Aberdeen appear in the records from the early 1130s, and in the dioceses of Brechin, Caithness, Dunblane and Moray the episcopal succession was established on a firmer footing by the late 1140s or earlier 1150s. The last diocese to be founded was one for which there was no earlier precedent, that of Argyll, which was eventually carved off from the unwieldy diocese of Dunkeld at some date between 1183 and 1188, in the reign of David's grandson, William the Lion.

The earliest surviving cathedral buildings

Putting aside the possibility of remains of St Ninian's church at Whithorn, the earliest surviving building associated with a cathedral church is probably the round tower embodied within the south-west corner of Brechin Cathedral, though it is doubtful how far Brechin was in any sense a cathedral rather than a monastic centre at the time the tower was built. This tower is one of the two free-standing cylindrical bell towers of Irish type known to have been built in Scotland (**2** and **colour plate 1**), the other being at Abernethy, which had itself possibly been a cathedral centre in the eighth century. The dating of these two towers is problematic, though the details of that at Abernethy suggest it was built in the late eleventh or early twelfth centuries, albeit with earlier masonry retained at its base. The Brechin tower was the more ambitious of the two, having a carved doorway with crouching beasts flanking the threshold, saints on the jambs and a crucifixion at the apex of the arch. The style of this doorway invites comparison with Irish work such as that on the high cross at Dysert O'Dea (Clare), which supports the interpretation that the tower is as late as the early twelfth century.

Problems of dating also bedevil our understanding of what is arguably the first surviving church built as a cathedral in Scotland, the building known as St Rule's at St Andrews (**3**). This was probably first erected as

2 Brechin Cathedral from the south-west, before the restoration of 1900–2. The early round tower can be seen at one corner of the west front, and the thirteenth-and-fourteenth-century tower at the other.

a three-compartment structure, two of which still survive. Most prominent is a very lofty square tower, with a tall rectangular compartment which is likely to have been intended as a nave to its east, beyond which there seems to have been a chancel. The whole building is constructed of large blocks of finely squared masonry known as ashlar. Several writers have suggested that these earliest parts of St Rule's date from the time of Bishop Fothad, who became bishop in about 1070, and that this was the one church said to be still in use at St Andrews at the time that Bishop Robert, who had been elected in 1124, was eventually consecrated in 1127. Support for so early a date has been drawn from the double-splayed windows in the flanks of the nave, which have arches constructed of coursed

3 The church of St Rule at St Andrews from the south-east. The arch through the east wall is clearly visible.

masonry or arched lintels rather than the radiating stones known as voussoirs, as well as from the way the arch between the tower and nave is constructed. Analogies for these details can be seen in English pre-Conquest architecture, while parallels for the planning might be drawn with fragmentary remains at Restenneth Priory in Angus, and with the excavated remains of a church built for St Margaret below the later abbey church of Dunfermline, in the place where she married Malcolm III in about 1070.

However, an alternative interpretation of the first parts of St Rule's is that both the planning and the quality of the masonry have closer parallels in churches that were being built for David I around the second quarter of the twelfth century, such as St Serf's Priory on Loch Leven, and Inchcolm Priory in the Firth of Forth. In this view, it is more likely that the church was built after Robert was elected bishop in 1124. Support for this might also be drawn from architectural parallels with the tower of Markinch parish church in Fife, which was a possession of St Andrews, and which may have been built by masons from St Andrews. Although there can be no certainty, on the whole the later date for St Rule's seems more likely, in which case it was presumably built in two phases by Bishop Robert as part of his attempt to modernize his diocese.

From the start, Bishop Robert was evidently intent on replacing the existing bodies of clergy at what was Scotland's most important episcopal centre by clergy who would be more in sympathy with his own reformist aims. He certainly cannot have been happy with those that he found at St Andrews: among various groups, one was of Culdees, whose members had apparently once been married, though they may have made other provision for their wives after they joined the order; another was a body of priests who perhaps still enjoyed the

company of wives and passed on their priestly functions to their sons. It seems that none of these clergy accepted responsibility for a full daily round of services. This situation was no longer acceptable and, since Robert had been prior of the recently founded house of Augustinian Canons at Scone before his election to St Andrews, it was natural that he regarded a priory of Augustinians as the ideal chapter for his new cathedral. But he had great difficulties in achieving this, and it was not until 1144 that he overcame the vested interests of the existing clergy and established the priory.

It was probably around the time the Augustinians were introduced that St Rule's was extended to provide a larger nave for the layfolk to the west of the tower, and perhaps also a longer eastern limb. These extensions have been destroyed and we are uncertain about their layout; nevertheless, two arches have survived that either had to be cut through the earlier fabric into the extensions or were simply remodellings of earlier openings. On the basis of their details, it has been suggested that the masons who designed these arches probably came from Yorkshire, and there are parallels with the church tower at Wharram-le-Street, to the north-east of York. This is of particular interest, because Wharram church was a possession of Nostell Priory in Yorkshire, where Bishop Robert had originally been a canon before he went to Scone. This suggests that Robert had sent to Nostell for masons to help him in his building operations.

St Rule's church is thus significant for what it tells us about the way that architectural ideas might be introduced at the start of a period of major architectural expansion. The first half of the twelfth century was to be a phase of seminal importance in the history of the Scottish Church and its architecture, because an unprecedented number of monasteries, parish churches and cathedrals were founded. Since there simply were not enough masons in Scotland to design and build all of these new churches, however, many craftsmen had to be brought in from elsewhere. Relationships with England, although frequently strained, were strong, and it was natural that help should be sought from there, particularly since England was one of the more architecturally advanced nations of Europe at this period. As with the new ideas being introduced for the organization of the church, a major influence behind all of this must have been David I who, as a prince living mainly in England before his accession, had evidently been interested in the latest architectural ideas being developed for the many new churches under construction south of the Border. At the abbey churches erected under his own direct patronage, such as Jedburgh, Kelso, Dunfermline and Holyrood, it seems he must have had firm ideas about which parts of England he wished to draw masons from to construct his new buildings, and it is likely he was also taking a keen interest in what was happening at some of the cathedrals.

One cathedral in which David probably took a special interest was that at Glasgow, where he had introduced his old tutor and friend, John, as bishop. For all that David I was a devoted son of the Church, he had a strong vision of the integrity of his kingdom, and one of his aims was to be rid of the claims of the archbishop of York to have authority over the Scottish Church. What he hoped to achieve was to have Scotland recognized as a separate province within the Church, with an archbishop at St Andrews, and John of Glasgow was the bishop charged with pursuing this. Though he was to be ultimately unsuccessful – only in 1472 did St Andrews eventually become an archbishopric – John and David continued to enjoy a close relationship. They were jointly involved in founding the Augustinian abbey of Jedburgh close to the Border with England in about 1138, and they may have similarly co-operated in the building of John's new cathedral at Glasgow, which was ready for dedication in 1136.

Nothing survives of John's church above ground, though a fragment of painted stone found in 1916 could be from continuing work on the cathedral after 1136 (a dedication does not necessarily imply that a building was complete so much as that it was ready for worship) (**colour plate 2**). However, excavations in 1992–3 located what may have been part of the west front of John's church, about one-third of the way down the nave of the later cathedral. Also found in these excavations were a number of re-used semi-circular stone drums from piers of relatively small scale, which probably came from John's church. They appear likely to have been either the supports of the vaulting of a crypt – the steep eastward fall of the land almost certainly meant that a crypt was necessary from the start – or the piers of small arcades separating the aisles from the main space of the church.

Another part of a cathedral of this period is represented by the lower four storeys of the tower embodied within the mid-thirteenth-century south aisle at Dunblane Cathedral (**4** and see **colour plate 6**). Since there are no signs of this tower having been attached originally to

4 Dunblane Cathedral nave from the south, with the Romanesque tower at the centre. The later heightening of the tower is evident in the change of colour of the stone.

another building, it seems it was a free-standing bell tower, probably with the church that it served to its north, since the only doorway in the tower is on the north side. Nothing is known of the church associated with this tower, apart from a few arch-stones with chevron (zig-zag) decoration preserved within the present cathedral. The tower is a relatively plain structure, and is divided into stages by string courses (projecting horizontal bands of stone). As at St Rule's, the greatest emphasis is on the paired windows of the top belfry stage, which in this case are of developed Romanesque form, having a semi-circular containing arch, with two sub-arches carried on a column set well back from the wall face. The ground-floor stage of the tower evidently contained a chapel covered by a ribbed barrel vault, with the altar within a semi-circular recess in the east wall.

The tower doorway is of a similar date as the belfry windows, and the rectangular opening is framed within a semi-circular arch, which had nook shafts with simple cushion capitals supporting the arch itself. The shafts have gone, though their capitals remain. Mention may be made here of a more richly decorated Romanesque doorway of about the same period which has been reset on the south side of the aisle-less nave at Whithorn (5 and see **colour plate 9**). This opening has four orders of mouldings to the round arch, which are decorated with chevron (zig-zag) or roundels, while the capitals of the engaged shafts carrying those orders are carved with a variety of motifs. If the details of St Rule's and Dunblane suggest the presence of English-trained masons, those of Whithorn could point to Irish masons having been behind the work. Here it should be remembered that at a time when transport by water could be easier than travelling across land, parts of western Scotland were more easily reached from Ireland than from either Lowland Scotland or England.

Dunblane's tower was possibly built in the time of Laurence, the first bishop recorded for the diocese, who is mentioned in 1161 and appears in other documents datable to between 1165 and 1171. There is evidence that some bishops of Dunblane might prefer to base themselves in the Strathearn district of their diocese, rather than in the Menteith part where Dunblane is situated. When in Strathearn they were presumably based at Muthill, which by the twelfth century was a Culdee centre, and had probably been one for some time before. Significantly, there is a tower at Muthill that is related to the one at Dunblane, perhaps suggesting there was simultaneous architectural activity in both places (**6**). As at Dunblane, Muthill's tower seems to have been originally free-standing, and the belfry windows were also similar (though two of those at Muthill have been rebuilt later along with wall-head gables); further similarities can be seen between the diamond-pattern decoration on the string course that runs around the lower storey at Muthill, and the similar pattern on the moulding that runs round the altar recess in the lower storey at Dunblane. Nevertheless, Muthill's tower is simpler than that at Dunblane, with a plan of only about 4.65m (15ft 3in) square as opposed to the 6.85m (22ft 6in) of Dunblane.

Another church probably used by the bishops of its diocese where it is again questionable how far it can be described specifically as a cathedral is at Birnie, in Moray. Before the diocese was fixed at Spynie in 1207–8 and finally at Elgin in 1224 (**colour plate 3**), the bishops of Moray moved around between Birnie, Spynie and Kinneddar. Little remains within the churchyards at Spynie and Kinneddar to indicate the erstwhile existence of cathedral churches (though Spynie still has its nearby episcopal castle); but at Birnie there is a mid-twelfth-century church, which remains in use for worship. It is a simple building of two rectangular compartments, one at the east end for the chancel, and the other, larger, one for the nave; the latter was shortened and a belfry built on the new west gable in 1734. The best original feature of the church is the round-arched opening between the nave and chancel,

5 The Romanesque doorway rebuilt in the south wall of the
nave at Whithorn Cathedral.

the inner order of which is carried on sturdy shafts, with capitals of scalloped form (7).

It is possible that the church at Mortlach would once have been similar to that at Birnie, if there is any basis in the tradition that Mortlach was used by the bishops of Aberdeen before their move to Aberdeen in about 1131. However, most of the medieval work now visible at Mortlach appears to be of the thirteenth century, and must date from the time when it had become a parish church.

The first phase of building Kirkwall Cathedral

From all of this, it is clear that churches used as cathedrals in the first years of the twelfth century were not buildings on the vast scale that we have come to associate with such use. Since several abbeys were already being built on a great scale by the second quarter of the twelfth century, and large buildings were thus technically feasible, this small-scale approach to the cathedrals was presumably because the

6 Muthill church tower from the north-west (Galletly, *Ancient towers and doorways*, 1896).

7 Details of the chancel arch at Birnie church (Galletly, *Ancient towers and doorways*, 1896).

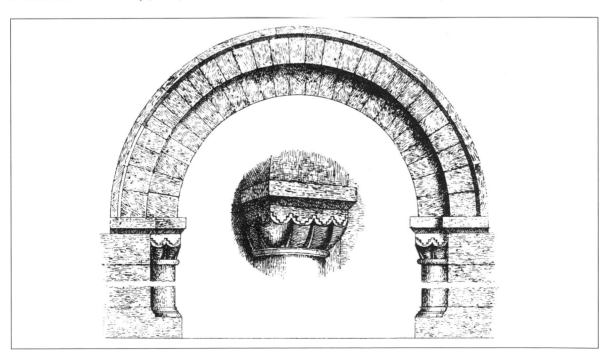

funds available to the dioceses were not yet sufficient to make more ambitious building possible. However, there is one major exception to this, Kirkwall in Orkney, where rebuilding was begun in about 1137, though it should be remembered that Kirkwall was not yet Scottish at the time the greater part of it was built, since the Northern Isles remained a possession of the kings of Norway until the fifteenth century.

Nevertheless, despite the fact that Kirkwall was probably the first of our cathedrals to be started on a grand scale, before it was built the bishops of Orkney are known to have used smaller churches as their cathedral. In the mid-eleventh century the cathedral was said to be at Birsay, though it is unclear if the church was on the site of the later parish church, or on the nearby tidal island known as the Brough of Birsay. On the Brough there are the lower walls of a church excavated in 1866 and again in the 1930s, which has a square chancel with an eastern semi-circular projection known as an apse, and a rectangular nave with provision for either a tower or porch at its western end. But this church is unlikely to date from before the early twelfth century and, if it was a church on the Brough that was used by the bishops, it is more likely to have been a structure of which slight remains have been found beneath the early twelfth-century church. As an alternative to the church on the Brough, the bishops could have used a church on the site of the parish church, of which traces were found through excavation at its east end in 1982. It may be mentioned here that one of the delights of Orkney is the rich variety of twelfth-century churches of which there are remains. One on the island of Egilsay, probably built to commemorate the murder in 1116 of St Magnus, Earl of Orkney, may also have been regarded in some way as a bishop's church. It has a two-storeyed rectangular chancel, a larger rectangular nave and a tall circular tower which is visible over a wide area.

The decision to build a new cathedral in Kirkwall was taken in about 1137 by Earl Rognvald of Orkney, the nephew of St Magnus, in the time of Bishop William (1112–68). Work was started on a massive project which expanded as the work progressed, but which was incomplete at the Reformation (**colour plate 4**). The original scale of the building was similar to that of the abbey church of Dunfermline as started by David I in about 1128. As usual, work commenced with the liturgically more important east end, so that those parts would be ready for the main services as soon as possible. So far as we now understand the first plan, it was for a relatively short eastern limb of two-and-a-half aisled bays, terminating in a semi-circular apse for the high altar and the shrine of St Magnus; externally the aisles flanking the main space apparently ended in straight walls, though these could have concealed internal apses. The short transepts (cross arms) were aisle-less, but probably initially had apses on their east face (see **36**). The aisled nave was eventually eight bays long, though it is uncertain if this was the original intention, and above the crossing of the four arms was a central tower (**8**).

Internally, as would be expected in a major church of this period, the church was of three storeys. At the lowest level, tall arcades opened into the stone-vaulted aisles, with round arches carried on cylindrical piers. At the intermediate level were round-arched openings into galleries between the stone vaults and the roofs over the aisles; these galleries were probably first intended to have high external walls with windows, but as eventually built the roofs swept steeply down, leaving no space for windows. At the top level was the clearstorey, with windows casting light into the central space, and with a passage in the thickness of the walls. Originally the cathedral had a timber roof or ceiling above the high main spaces, though stone vaulting was introduced at a later stage, and this is one illustration of the way the work became more ambitious as it progressed. In the earlier phases this increasingly ambitious approach is seen in the introduction of a decorative band of arcading below the lowest level of windows in the transepts and nave aisles, whereas the lower walls of the choir had been plain.

As with the plan, many details of the earlier work at Kirkwall are related to those at Dunfermline Abbey and, as at Dunfermline, it is tempting to suspect that masons from Durham Cathedral were involved in the design. In some ways Kirkwall is slightly closer in spirit to Durham than is Dunfermline, because Kirkwall's decorative arcading has intersecting arches, whereas Dunfermline's has single arches. But Kirkwall was in no sense a straight copy of either, and in the superimposition of tier upon tier of round arches there is also something of the same spirit that is to be seen at Carlisle Cathedral in Cumberland. In this respect it is important to remember that the Norwegian Church, of which Kirkwall was still a part, was much influenced by what was happening in England, and ideas could have been drawn from a wide range of buildings.

The massively constructed work of the first phases of Kirkwall is entirely Romanesque in spirit, with its heavy sense of the weight of the wall, its round arches and its capitals of the types known as cushion or scalloped. However, in further changes that were to be introduced before the transepts had been completed, we see a new spirit entering the work. For some reason it was decided to rebuild the piers that support the central tower, and the chapels on the east side of the transepts were remodelled to a rectangular plan, while soon afterwards a doorway was cut through the south wall of the south transept. In all of this, the moulded and

8 The interior of the nave of Kirkwall Cathedral from the south-west.

carved stonework is treated rather differently from that in the previous work. The mouldings have become thinner and more attenuated, and many of them have pointed profiles, all of which creates a lighter and more linear impression than widely rounded forms. At the same time, the visually heavy cushion and scalloped capitals were superseded by two new types of capital. In one, the body of the capital is covered by broad fleshy leaves which curl upwards at the corners; these are known as water-leaf capitals. In the other, there are similar large leaves over the capital as a whole, but the foliage develops outwards and downwards at the angles, forming what are known as crockets. Another change is that the arches of the transept chapel windows, of the south doorway, and those over the crossing piers, are all pointed.

These changes seem unlikely to date from before the last decades of the twelfth century, and it is possible they correspond with a new impetus being given to the work following the election of Bishop Biarne Kolbeinsson in 1188. However, at this stage it is probably best to postpone consideration of the continuing work at Kirkwall in order to look at what was the most important church building operation started on mainland Scotland in the second half of the twelfth century.

The start of building at St Andrews Cathedral

Construction of the new cathedral at St Andrews was started while Arnold was bishop, between 1160 and 1162. He was well used to building operations because he had been head of the Tironensian abbey of Kelso, in the Borders, where construction was started in about 1128 and was still in progress. As the cathedral of bishops who claimed supremacy in Scotland and independence of York, it was important that his new church at St Andrews should make a clear statement of dominance, and it was by far the largest church ever planned in Scotland. The plan of its eastern arm was an expansion on a type that had perhaps been first developed

coherently for Archbishop Thomas of York's Southwell Minster in Nottinghamshire between 1108 and 1114. In this plan type, which had already been taken up in Scotland at Jedburgh in about 1138 as well as in a number of other English churches, a square-ended aisle-less eastern section projects beyond an aisled choir. But at St Andrews this plan was extended beyond what was usual, with an aisle-less section of two bays beyond an aisled section of six bays (see 89). The aisle-less section was probably originally intended as a presbytery for the high altar, but it later became a shrine or relic chapel. West of the aisled choir were transepts, each four bays wide, with chapels on their east side, and the nave was probably originally intended to be fourteen bays long, though it was eventually built with only twelve.

Despite St Andrews Cathedral being now in a very ruined state, enough survives to have an idea of what its eastern parts must have looked like internally. The main space was, of course, three storeys high, with tall arches opening into the aisled sections; above that was an unusually high gallery stage of rather more than half the height of the arcades. The clearstorey stage at the top was possibly modified in course of building, because the decision was taken to cover the high central space as well as the aisles with stone vaulting, and the three arches on the inner skin of the wall passage were stepped to fit in with the arches of the vault (see 10). To get some idea of how it all must have appeared, we may look to the nave of Jedburgh Abbey, which was started in the last quarter of the century, and which was probably designed by masons who had worked earlier at St Andrews, though Jedburgh had vaults only over the aisles.

The design of St Andrews is of outstanding importance for our understanding of the development and spread of architectural ideas at this period. It was almost certainly devised by masons from northern England, and it seems likely that it gave them opportunities to work on an even grander scale than would have been possible in northern England at that time. Some

9 The surviving lower part of the west wall of the south transept at St Andrews Cathedral, showing the intersecting arcading and round-headed windows.

of the ideas we see had been in circulation for a while. There was intersecting arcading along the lower walls of the unaisled section of the choir (now gone) and of the transepts (surviving in part), which was essentially a more up-to-date version of what we have already seen at Kirkwall (9 and see 8). The design of the great east wall, which terminated the vista down the church, originally had three tiers of triplets of round-headed windows, and this was also an idea that had been seen in some of the great English Romanesque cathedrals, though here it was treated in a more up-to-date manner (10). However, many other details of the design were absolutely in the vanguard of architectural fashion, and some of them show the influence of

ideas that had been introduced to northern England by Cistercian monks from Burgundy in eastern France.

It may seem strange that a particularly reclusive and austere order such as the Cistercians should have had such a great impact on architecture. But the earlier generations of the order laid great stress on architectural simplicity, and in an effort to retain it, as they spread across Europe, they took with them many of the architectural ideas with which they were familiar in eastern France, though these were inevitably intermingled with elements from the areas in which they took root. The ideas originating in eastern France included the use of pointed arches, and motifs such as piers made up of what appeared to be bundles of eight or more shafts, some or all of which were keeled (pointed); another motif they had made their own was the simple water-leaf capital, like those

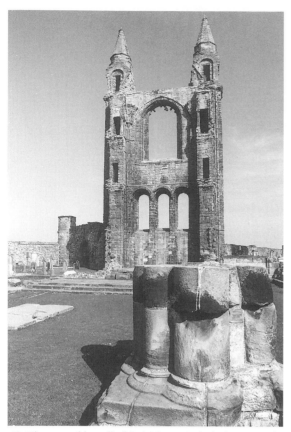

10 The east gable wall of St Andrews Cathedral. Traces of the two upper triplets of windows can be seen around the large fifteenth-century window. In the foreground is the lower part of one of the clustered-shaft piers of the choir arcades.

which the Cistercians built, as abbeys were founded for them across Yorkshire and the other English northern counties. Churches such as those at Fountains, Kirkstall, Roche and Byland presented a markedly different appearance from what had been customary in those areas, with their pointed arches, more sharply modelled mouldings and simplified details. In their turn they were to be highly influential on non-Cistercian churches, such as Archbishop Roger of York's collegiate church at Ripon, around the early 1160s, and apparently also on the magnificent choir that he was adding to his cathedral at York at about the same time (of which little now survives).

From what we can understand of the remains at St Andrews, it seems to have embodied many of those same ideas at a very early date. The relative proportions of the three storeys at St Andrews may well have been inspired by those of the cathedral at York, though this may seem a little perverse at the church of a bishop who was taking the lead in rejecting the claims of the archbishops of York. It is also worth noting that it was possibly at St Andrews that features such as bundled-shaft piers and capitals of water-leaf or crocket form were first used in a major Scottish church (see **10**), though this architectural vocabulary was soon to be developed more widely on both sides of the Border, in buildings which included Jedburgh and Arbroath in Scotland, and Hexham and Lanercost in northern England. As we have already seen, it was also to be reflected by the last decades of the century in the changes introduced at Kirkwall.

we have already encountered in the late twelfth-century work at Kirkwall. But underlying such details was an approach to design which gave many of their buildings an appearance of being more rigorously and economically engineered. All of this was to be reflected in the churches

2
The thirteenth century

Whithorn and Brechin Cathedrals

For reasons that are probably linked with the way diocesan finances were beginning to be placed on a better footing, the thirteenth century witnessed a remarkable outburst of cathedral building. Much of this new wealth came through the appropriation of large numbers of parishes, as landholders were increasingly encouraged to grant their rights in their local parish churches to a religious institution such as a cathedral or monastery. Once this had been done the body to which the parish had been granted usually appropriated the greater part of the parish's teinds (a tenth of its produce) to its own uses, setting aside enough to pay for a vicar or chaplain to meet the spiritual needs of the parishioners.

Starting with one of the less completely understood operations, at Whithorn, rebuilding of the eastern parts for the bishop and Premonstratensian canons is thought to have begun in about 1200, though much of what we know of it comes from accounts of excavations in the late nineteenth century for the Marquess of Bute, and from the heavily consolidated walls that were left exposed. It is one possibility that the new eastern limb was a smaller version of the one at St Andrews, with an unaisled section projecting east of an aisled choir presumably for a chapel for the shrine of St Ninian, and with transepts between choir and nave (see **90**). But, if this was indeed the arrangement, we do not know if the unaisled section rose to the same

height as the rest of the main spaces, or if it was lower. Smaller lateral off-shoots projected asymmetrically from both the north-east and south-east sides of the eastern limb, that on the south possibly having been a Lady Chapel and that on the north perhaps a two-storeyed sacristy and treasury block. Some of these offshoots could post-date a fire referred to in the register of the archbishops of York in 1286, while further works were in progress in the time of Bishop Alexander Vaus (1422–50). In 1423, for example, the Earl of Douglas and his wife provided endowments for the construction and endowment of a chapel, while some work was still in progress in 1428 when the priory was ordered to contribute half of its income to the work. The barrel vaults below the far east end of the building are assumed to have been rebuilt around 1500, and money for work on the cathedral was still being received on the very eve of the Reformation.

Mercifully, other early thirteenth-century cathedral building operations are less enigmatic than Whithorn's, though at both Brechin and Dornoch post-Reformation destruction followed by over-eager rebuilding and restoration have reduced our understanding. At Brechin, apart from the early round tower at the south-west corner of the nave and some later modifications, the cathedral was substantially of the thirteenth century. The nave is a relatively simple two-storeyed design, with no stone vaulting over either the main space or the aisles. Its five aisled

11 The interior of the nave of Brechin Cathedral, looking towards the choir. The south arcade is on the right and the north arcade on the left (Crown Copyright: Royal Commission on the Ancient and Historical Monument of Scotland).

bays, with chapels at the east end of each aisle, have arcades of pointed arches; that on the south side has octagonal piers, while the piers of the north arcade alternate between octagonal and more complex forms (11 and see 77). One of those more complex piers has slender roll mouldings cut into the angles of the basic octagon, and this relates it to types at Arbroath Abbey and Hexham Priory (Northumberland), suggesting a date not much later than about 1200. A relatively early date is supported by the other elaborated pier, which is of the bundled-shaft type already referred to at St Andrews as having been introduced into Britain by the Cistercians in the second half of the twelfth century. The responds (half-piers) at the east end of the arcades are also of this type.

Unfortunately, the bases of the piers, which might have helped to date the nave more closely, appear to have been recut at the time of a remodelling in 1806 which made the nave into more of a preaching hall. (This operation also involved raising the aisle walls and roofs in a utilitarian style and enclosing the clearstorey within the building, though a later restoration by John Honeyman in 1900–2 re-exposed it.) The small windows of the clearstorey are set above the piers rather than above the arch heads, giving the nave an appearance similar to Crail parish church in Fife, and reminding us that the cathedral is of little more than parochial scale. The finest single feature of the nave was perhaps the last part of this phase of works to be completed. This was the doorway in the west front, which has a widely splayed progression of finely moulded orders of arches, carried on no less than five shafts alternating with other mouldings. This was amongst the earliest of a series of ever-more ambitious west doorways to be built as the processional entrances to the cathedrals. A rather less imposing main entrance for layfolk was usually provided in the south wall of the nave, but at Brechin it was on the north. The north and south walls of the nave aisles, along with the flanking chapels and porch, are now largely inventions of the 1900 restoration.

The choir, which is of slightly later construction than the nave, was abandoned after the Reformation but, as part of the 1900 restoration (by which time little of it remained standing), it was rebuilt to a shortened plan (**12**). Despite its incomplete and heavily restored state, the choir can still be appreciated as an elegant design, with lancets (tall pointed windows) within a continuous arcade carried on triplets of shafts. This is a related approach to what was to be done in the choirs of Beauly

12 Brechin Cathedral from the south-east.

31

Priory (Inverness-shire), started in about 1230, and Dornoch Cathedral, which was started soon after 1222. In view of these dates, is it possible that building of Brechin's choir coincided with the attempts of Bishop Gregory (1218–42) to transform a community of Culdees into a chapter of secular canons?

As originally planned, Brechin seems not to have been intended to have a bell tower other than the early round tower, but one was eventually started at the west end of the north aisle (see **2** and **colour plate 1**). Its lower storey was covered by stone vaulting, which is carried on shafts bearing capitals decorated with the type of luxuriantly formalized windblown foliage known rather inappropriately as stiff-leaf. The variant on this foliage seen at Brechin is unlikely to be earlier than the mid-thirteenth century.

Dornoch Cathedral and the first phase of Elgin Cathedral

The cathedral of Caithness diocese was moved from Halkirk to Dornoch by Bishop Gilbert de Moravia (1222–45), and building was presumably started soon after the move. It was

14 The interior of the choir and crossing of Dornoch Cathedral (Crown Copyright: Royal Commission on the Ancient and Historical Monuments of Scotland).

13 The choir, transepts and central tower of Dornoch Cathedral from the east.

set out to a cruciform plan, with rectangular aisle-less choir and transepts of approximately equal size, and with a low tower and spire over the crossing (**13** and see **78**). The choir is lit by groups of three lancets in each of its external walls and, in a slightly simpler variant of the idea already seen at Brechin, they are interconnected by a continuous arcade originally carried on shafts (**14**). The main problem at Dornoch is to know what the nave was like.

The present nave is aisle-less and dates from a restoration by Alexander Coupar of 1835–7; until then it had been in a ruined state following the burning of the whole building in 1570, having been left to continue decaying when the other parts were progressively repaired from 1614 onwards. However, it seems that the nave in its only recorded state was four or five bays long, with an aisle down each side. The main survivors of this are the partial remains of the responds (half-piers) at the east end of the nave arcades, where they joined the piers below the tower. These responds have shafts with raised strips known as fillets, and are likely to have been designed later than the tower piers themselves, though not necessarily much later. We also have a rather inaccurate late-eighteenth-century view of the nave which shows that the south arcade had cylindrical piers, and that the low clearstorey had windows over the arch heads (**15**). This view also shows small round-headed windows in the unvaulted aisles, but a massive five-light window with intersecting tracery in the west wall. It has been suggested by some writers that the nave as shown in that view dates from the later Middle Ages, and comparisons have been made with the nave of Aberdeen. Yet, while it is certain that the west window must be considerably more recent than the choir, it could be an insertion in an earlier structure, since there is much in Dornoch's nave that looks like that of Brechin, and could equally be of the thirteenth century. Unfortunately, there can be no certainty on the evidence we now have.

If the aisled nave of Dornoch had been a continuation of the early thirteenth-century scheme, the basic form of the building would have been comparable with that of the new cathedral of the diocese of Moray at Elgin, which was under construction in the same years

15 The nave of Dornoch Cathedral in about 1776 (Cordiner, *Remarkable ruins and romantic prospects of North Britain*, 1795).

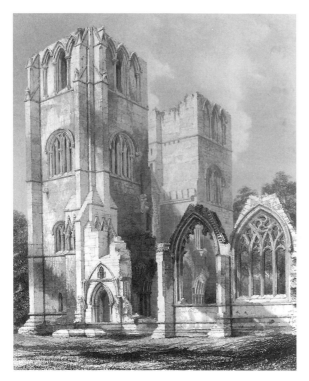

16 The south wall of the nave and the west towers of Elgin Cathedral (Billings, *The baronial and ecclesiastical antiquities of Scotland*, 1845–52).

that St Gilbert was at work in Dornoch. Elgin was started when papal permission was given to move the diocese from Spynie to Elgin on 10 April 1224 and, as at Dornoch, the original scheme was for an aisle-less rectangular eastern limb and aisle-less transepts. The aisled nave was probably originally planned to be of six bays. However, at Elgin the design expanded in the course of the work, and it was decided to add an imposing pair of symmetrical western towers to supplement a central tower over the crossing of main spaces and transepts (16 and colour plate 3). Another addition was a three-bay chapel against the south flank of the nave, at its junction with the transept.

As a result of later rebuilding, little remains of this first campaign apart from the western towers and south transept. The transept gable wall is a satisfyingly simple composition (17), with a doorway and a pair of lancet windows at the lower level, and a triplet of round-headed windows at the upper level, the latter opening on to an internal wall passage. It is an interesting aspect of this design that the round-headed windows must be later than the pointed ones: a reversal of what is usually expected, and a reminder that round and pointed arches could be used interchangeably in the earlier thirteenth century. The western towers rise through four storeys, becoming progressively lighter in appearance as they rise higher (see 16 and colour plate 3). At the lower level are tiny single lancets, above which are small two-light windows, with four-light windows at the third level; the top stage has large single openings within a continuous decorative arcade. The towers were probably originally capped by lead and timber spires.

Little survives of the main spaces of the cathedral as first built, though it is clear the nave was of two storeys, with arcades opening into the flanking aisles, and an upper level of clearstorey windows with a passage towards the interior like that in the south transept. Internally the choir may have had a continuous arcade embracing windows at the higher level as at Dornoch. There was originally no stone vaulting over either the aisles or the higher main spaces, the only vaulting from this phase of works being in the towers. The piers supporting the arches of the nave arcades were of a type that was beginning to be popular in Scotland at this period, with engaged shafts (the main ones being keeled, or pointed) set into a basically stepped plan, a type that had already been used in the parts of Holyrood Abbey nave started in about 1210, and that was soon to be used in several other major churches.

A particularly intriguing feature which survives from a later phase of this first building campaign is the fragmentary remains of a rose window (18), which probably came from the terminal wall of either the choir or nave. This suggests that although the part of the building it was made for was subsequently remodelled or

17 The south transept of Elgin Cathedral.

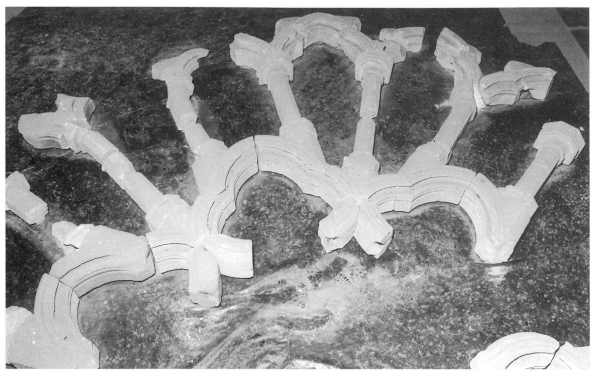

18 Fragments of a rose window from an unknown location in Elgin Cathedral.

destroyed, the stones of the window were saved for some other use. The details of the window indicate it was designed by craftsmen who made similar windows in northern England, at Byland Abbey, York Minster and elsewhere, and which are datable to around the central decades of the thirteenth century.

Glasgow Cathedral

The most instructive of the cathedrals for what it can tell us about thirteenth-century architecture is at Glasgow (19). In a series of operations starting in the last decades of the twelfth century and continuing with few pauses beyond the end of the thirteenth century, the whole building was reconstructed on a scale surpassed only by St Andrews. It has survived largely complete apart from its western towers, and provides incomparable evidence within one high-quality building for the way attitudes to design developed in the course of one of the most architecturally productive periods of the Middle Ages.

The earliest fragment remaining in place in the cathedral is a short spur of wall, with an attached shaft surmounted by a capital with simple stiff-leaf decoration, near the south-west corner of the crypt (20). This fragment almost certainly belongs to a building campaign initiated by Bishop Jocelin (1174–99), and was presumably part of a transept-like projection which belonged to an extension around the east end of the building that had been dedicated by Bishop John in 1136. Jocelin was an active promoter of the cult of St Kentigern, and it is likely his extension was aimed at providing a more appropriate setting for the saint's tomb at crypt level. Beyond that, as a culmination to the struggle with the archbishops of York, it was in Jocelin's time that Pope Alexander III placed the diocese, and soon afterwards the whole Scottish Church, under the pope's special care rather than within the province of York. This may have encouraged the bishop to give his cathedral a more dignified form with greater space for the high altar and canons' choir at the main level.

19 Glasgow Cathedral from the south-east.

20 The south-west compartment of the crypt at Glasgow Cathedral, with the shaft surviving from Bishop Jocelin's late twelfth-century church on the right.

Excavations in 1992–3 indicated that Jocelin also started to rebuild the nave to an aisle-less plan, though this part of his work cannot have progressed very far. The chronicle compiled at the abbey of Melrose, of which Jocelin had earlier been abbot, recorded that he was building at Glasgow in 1181 and there was a dedication in 1197, but it seems work was interrupted by a fire and may never have been completed before his death in 1199.

There may then have been a hiatus of building activity over a period when no bishop held the diocese for any extended period, and it seems that work was only reactivated in the early years of the thirteenth century, possibly in the time of Bishop Walter (1207–32). When work did start again, Jocelin's transeptal projection, which was possibly still unfinished, was cut off by the wall of a new aisle (the one we still see) and as an extension of the same process non-projecting transepts were laid out to the west of where Jocelin's transepts had been; following this, the outer walls of the present nave were laid out. In all of this a division of the interior into regular bays was marked by single wall shafts of keeled (pointed) section which were intended to support vaulting in the crypt and the nave aisles.

However, yet again before work could be completed there was a further change of plan, and in 1242 the faithful throughout the kingdom were exhorted to contribute to further rebuilding at Glasgow (**21**). The prime mover behind this was Bishop William Bondington

21 The south elevation of the choir and transept of Glasgow Cathedral (Collie, *Plans, elevations ... and views of the cathedral of Glasgow*, 1835).

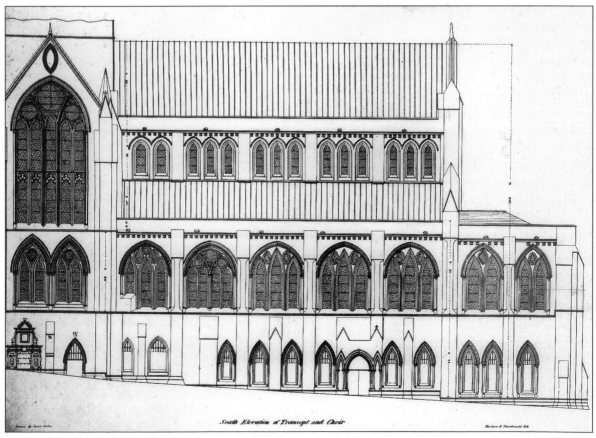

South Elevation of Transept and Choir

(1233–58). During his episcopate the chapter of dignitaries and secular canons that served the cathedral was beginning to take more settled form, and it was eventually agreed by the end of Bondington's episcopate that the constitution of Salisbury Cathedral was to provide a basis for Glasgow's chapter. This was presumably a deliberate revival of a link forged a hundred years earlier, when Bishop Herbert had adopted the early twelfth-century Sarum customs (constitution) for his cathedral clergy. Once more, it seems, the existing choir had been deemed inadequate for the cathedral's expanding dignity. Bondington's new eastern limb was planned to be large enough to house a spacious presbytery around the high altar, a shrine chapel for St Kentigern, and it could also accommodate the whole of the canons' choir. Thus, as was perhaps already the case at St Andrews, all of these functions were to be fully contained within an architecturally distinct limb of the building. As with the earlier churches on the site, however, the fall of the land meant the new eastern limb had to be raised above a crypt, which was now planned to provide a setting for the saint's tomb (**22**, and see **84** and **85**).

To meet all these needs, Bondington's architect adopted a plan possibly first developed in England at the turn of the eleventh and twelfth centuries, but which had then been further developed by the Cistercians as a way of incorporating space for a considerable number of altars within a relatively simple framework (see **colour plate 5**). In this plan there were aisles down each side of the main space, and at the east end of the main space they were interconnected by a third aisle at right angles to the others, beyond which there was a straight row of chapels, rising no higher than the aisle. The main plan was thus contained within a rectangle, though at Glasgow a number of laterally projecting structures were tacked on around it. On the north side, at the eastern corner, a two-storeyed chapter house block was built, with vaulting carried on a central pier at both levels, while a two-storeyed treasury and

22 The area around the site of St Kentigern's tomb in the crypt of Glasgow Cathedral.

sacristy block was placed against the western bay of the north aisle (the upper storey of this has been destroyed). Probably only a little later, a widely projecting two-storeyed chapel was started against the south transept. This perhaps covered the supposed site of the burial of the holy man called Fergus, whose hearse Kentigern was said to have followed to Glasgow, since Fergus's body and hearse were represented on the later vault over the aisle.

The beauty of the main elements of this plan was that they allowed access for pilgrims to all points of interest, including a shrine chapel behind the high altar, without disturbing the services of the canons. But there was the potential disadvantage at crypt level that by extending the building eastwards, the site of the tomb was left at an uncomfortably undefined point. It was in response to this that the master mason showed his genius. He created an additional focus in the crypt by placing the second most important subsidiary chapel in the cathedral, the Lady Chapel (dedicated to the Virgin Mary), at the east end of the main space, over which he placed a slightly domed section of vaulting. This left Kentigern's tomb near the centre of the remaining space and, by carefully positioning the piers which supported the surrounding vaulting, he concentrated attention on the site of the tomb with what was effectively a vaulted canopy supported by four richly decorated piers (see **22**). Although changes in the architectural details suggest this solution was evolved only over a period of some years, it represents an extraordinarily advanced piece of spatial modelling which was hardly to be echoed again in Britain before the end of the century.

At the main level of the new eastern arm, the likely origins of the master mason are indicated by the way he devised a design (**23** and **colour plate 5**) that seems to have been ultimately inspired by one of the more recent developments on a basic theme worked out at Lincoln

23 The interior of the choir at Glasgow Cathedral.

Cathedral. The choir there had been started in 1192, and work had extended down into the nave by the time that Glasgow was started. A more immediate inspiration for Glasgow may have been a building such as Rievaulx Abbey in Yorkshire, where the new choir was probably started around 1220, although the Glasgow master mason clearly was aware also of continuing developments at Lincoln itself. As at those buildings, Glasgow has a three-storeyed design, and it is particularly in the middle storey, the triforium, that parallels with Rievaulx are to be seen in the use of two pairs of openings in each bay, with each pair contained by its own arch. The main difference between Glasgow and the buildings that influenced its design is that while the latter had stone vaults over both their aisles and the high main space of their choirs, Glasgow was given vaults only over the aisles and eastern chapels, and a timber wagon (pointed-section) ceiling was placed over the central space.

In suggesting some of the places from which the designer of Glasgow probably took his inspiration, it must not be thought that Glasgow was simply a derivative building. No work of architecture, however innovative, can be produced in creative isolation, and if we are to understand a building we must try to appreciate what part it played in the interchange of ideas between master masons. Glasgow was no slavish copy of any other building, as is seen in the way that some ideas coming to be favoured in Scotland also found a place there. One illustration of this is the pier design of the main arcades, which have engaged shafts (the main ones with a fillet like those already referred to at Dornoch) within a stepped overall plan; this was a type that was not common in England, but which, as already seen, had been used earlier in the nave of Elgin Cathedral. The design of Glasgow's top storey, the clearstorey, also had to depart from the prototype of Rievaulx's choir, since there was no vaulting to necessitate

an arched arrangement of openings. In this case the designing mason may have taken some ideas for the groupings of equal-height arches from the slightly earlier clearstorey in the nave at Jedburgh Abbey, which was in the diocese of Glasgow and under the patronage of its bishops, though the unvaulted south transept at Rievaulx also has a related type of clearstorey. The pointed timber roof which surmounted Glasgow's clearstorey was of delicately broken profile and, like its modern replacement, was decorated with a pattern of ribs.

Two noteworthy features of Glasgow are the foliage carving of the more important capitals and the designs of the windows, both of which may have been partly influenced by Lincoln. The foliage decoration includes some of the most inventively spirited stiff-leaf carving to be found in Scotland, though it recently has been discovered that parts of it were heavily restored in plaster in nineteenth-century restorations (24).

The windows are fascinating for the way they demonstrate in one building the rapidly changing fashions of the central decades of the century (25 and see 21). In the crypt we see some of the ways in which lancet windows could be used: there are single lancet windows, paired lancets and paired lancets within embracing arches. In the choir aisles we see the next stage of design, of which the thinner section of wall between the heads of the lancets and the embracing arch is pierced by small additional openings (almost as if by over-sized pastry-cutters); this is known as plate tracery, because the holes are cut through relatively thin plates of stone. At Glasgow we have one of the best groups of plate tracery anywhere in Britain, though it may have been inspired ultimately by the triforium openings in the nave at Lincoln. The next stage of tracery design is in the transepts, where work was evidently nearing completion in 1277, if a grant of timber to the bell tower is assumed to refer to the central tower. At this point bar tracery is introduced, in which the openings within the arch at the window head are defined by curved bars of

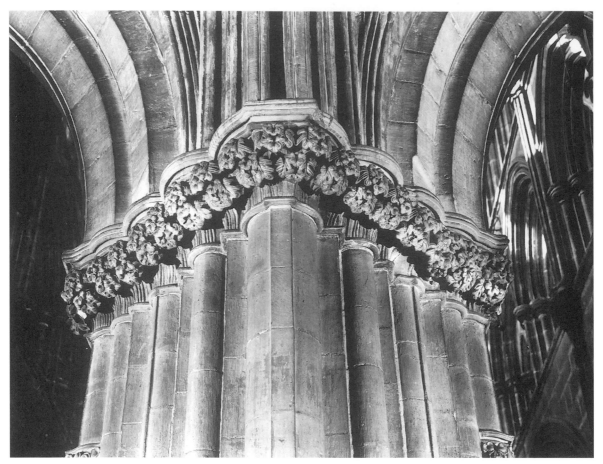

24 Stiff-leaf foliage on one of the choir arcade capitals in Glasgow Cathedral.

25 A simplified sketch of some of the window types in the choir of Glasgow Cathedral: A. Paired lancets. B. Paired lancets within embracing arches. C and D. Plate tracery. E. Bar tracery (author).

stone, rather than being simple piercings through plates of stone. Tracery of this sort had emerged in the royal domain of France around 1210, and had reached the English royal workshops at Westminster Abbey in about 1245. Assuming that work on the transepts was started around the 1260s, Glasgow must have been one of the first Scottish buildings to have such tracery. At the same time as tracery was designed for the transept windows, it was also

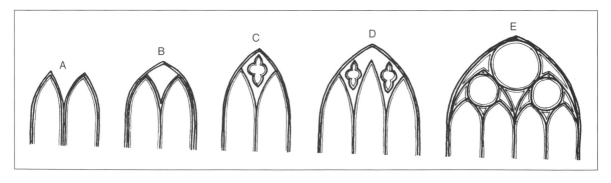

built into a window on the south side of the choir, which had probably been left open to allow materials to be hoisted to the upper parts of the eastern limb while work was still in progress. In these earlier bar-traceried windows the designs are made up of groupings of arches and circlets.

Work was restarted on the nave while the transepts were being completed. The magnificent processional west doorway, with its multiple-shafted orders and its division into two openings by a trumeau (central pier), looks to be of the central decades of the century, while the heavily restored window above it has tracery related to that in the transepts (see **27**). But the design that was developed for the interior of the nave was very different from that in the choir or transepts, and must have been the work of a new master mason (**26**). This change of design was necessitated partly because the positions of the shafts along the outer walls, which had been started soon after 1200, required narrower bays than in the choir. In responding to this the mason chose to emphasize the narrowness and verticality of the bays by connecting the two upper storeys with pairs of arches in each bay, which embraced both the upper stages of triforium and clearstorey.

Interconnection of the upper stages was an idea that had been around for many years; one of the earliest examples must have been the Welsh cathedral of St Davids, dating from the end of the twelfth century, and this might lead one to wonder if something similar had been intended for the nave of Glasgow when it was started in the early 1200s. However, this same idea of interconnecting the upper storeys had been developed in a number of different ways in the following decades, in places as far apart as Christchurch Cathedral in Dublin, Pershore Abbey (Worcestershire) and Southwell Minster (Nottinghamshire). One of the aims behind these experiments was to reduce the horizontal impact of the middle storey by making it seem like an extension of the clearstorey, and not long after the work on Glasgow's nave was

restarted there were to be even more sophisticated French-inspired experiments on the same theme in the nave of York Minster in the 1290s. While none of these provides precise parallels for Glasgow's nave, collectively they help us to appreciate the climate of thought within which it was designed.

The date of completion of Glasgow's nave is uncertain. However, several details, including window tracery in which there is a greater freedom of design through the absence of containing circlets, suggest the masonry shell was finished by the last years of the century. Nevertheless, the final works may have dragged on into the next century, because in 1306 Bishop Robert Wishart was accused of using timber intended for a bell tower to build siege engines as part of the Scottish resistance to the English King Edward I in the course of the Wars of Independence. This turning of ploughshares into swords may have been in connection with work on the northern tower of the two which used to flank the west front until the 1840s (**27**). When this tower was demolished it was seen that it blocked a window that had never been glazed, suggesting it was added as an afterthought once the rest of the nave was nearing completion, and early views of it certainly suggest its lower storeys were close in date to the nave. Its initial relationship with the cathedral would have been like that of the single north-west tower added to Brechin, and also similar to a tower added to Dunkeld in the fifteenth century (see **2, 47**). But at Glasgow it was eventually decided to add a second west tower, apparently in the fifteenth century, giving the cathedral three towers in all, though the southern one of the two seems never to have been completed.

Dunblane Cathedral and the earlier parts of Fortrose and Dunkeld Cathedrals

Apart from Glasgow, the most complete thirteenth-century cathedral is Dunblane, though its present completeness is a result of late-nineteenth-century reroofing of the nave

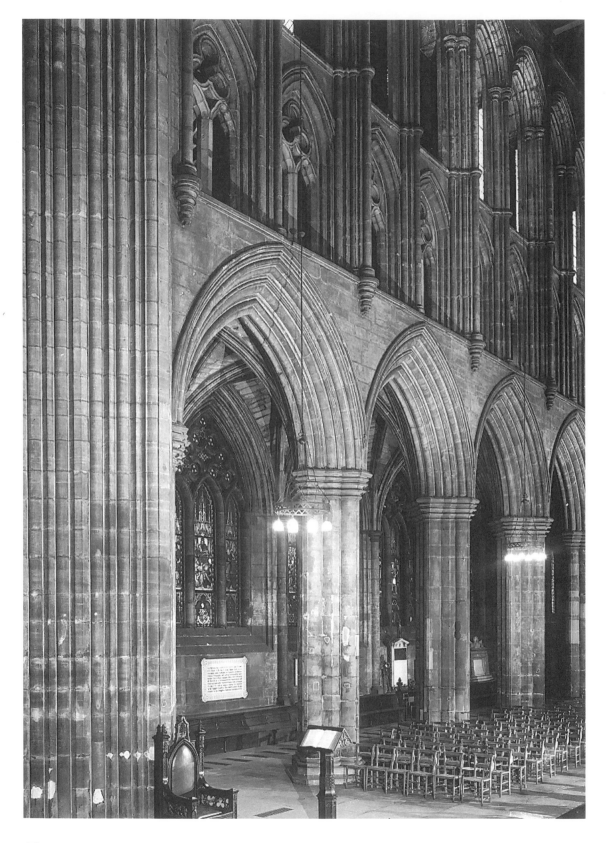

26 The interior of the nave at Glasgow Cathedral.

27 The west front of Glasgow Cathedral before the demolition of the west towers (Collie, *Plans, elevations ... and views of the cathedral of Glasgow*, 1835).

(see **33**, **70**). Reconstruction of the cathedral was started for Bishop Clement (1233–58), a member of the order of Dominican friars which had recently been introduced to Scotland. But before work could begin, the bishop had to show great determination to succeed, because he found the diocese in disarray, with much of its income misappropriated by local landowners, the existing cathedral roofless, and only one rural chaplain to serve it. To rectify this, on 11 June 1237 the pope commissioned the bishops of Glasgow and Dunkeld to look into the finances of the diocese and the staffing of the cathedral. In the course of this, thought was given to transferring the cathedral to the Augustinian abbey of Inchaffray, but it

eventually proved possible to sort out the situation at Dunblane. It was probably by the early 1240s that a chapter of secular canons was beginning to take shape, and perhaps around the same time that the cathedral began to be rebuilt.

We cannot be entirely certain about the progress of rebuilding Dunblane Cathedral, because of changes made since the Reformation, and also because several historically inappropriate details were introduced in a restoration of 1816–19 by James Gillespie Graham. A more scholarly restoration by Sir Robert Rowand Anderson in 1889–93 brought the abandoned nave back into use, and gave the choir a more authentic appearance, though by then there was little evidence for the original tracery of the choir windows. In consequence, we must be cautious in interpreting the architecture; but, on the evidence of the base courses, it seems the whole building was laid out in one operation, incorporating the twelfth-century tower, referred to in Chapter 1, within the south aisle of the nave (**28**; and see **79**). The eastern limb, for the presbytery and canons' choir, was an elongated rectangle, divided into six bays by buttresses, with a two-storeyed range along all but the eastern bay of its north flank to contain the sacristy, chapter house and treasury. The eight-bay nave had aisles along both sides, and a porch over the principal entrance for layfolk against the second and third bays from the east of the south aisle, adjacent to the retained tower. It is possible that an existing, smaller, choir was retained in use for a while when reconstruction started so that services were not interrupted, and the most likely building sequence may have been the chapter house block first, with the nave next and the new choir last. It is unlikely that the whole operation was completed much before the last decades of the thirteenth century, possibly in the time of Bishop Robert de Prebenda (1259–84).

The chapter house range has stone vaulting over its lower storey, with groupings of lancet

28 Dunblane Cathedral from the north-east. The choir is to the left, with the chapter house range running along its lower part; the nave is to the right.

windows in its north and east walls (29; and see 28). The aisles of the nave were probably started next, and they have similar windows, albeit on a larger scale, though the side windows of the east bay in each aisle were even larger to light the gabled chapels in those bays. The nave arcade piers were presumably started along with the aisle walls and, like the piers already referred to at Elgin and Glasgow, were variants on the type with engaged shafts within a basically stepped profile, though in the south arcade the angles of the steps were chamfered (see 31). However, before work was far advanced, there seems to have been the first of a number of changes of design. As we have seen at Brechin, Dornoch and Elgin, cathedral aisles were not invariably covered with stone vaulting, but in a building of the high quality of Dunblane vaults would

certainly be more normal. Since they had already been placed over the chapter house range it seems particularly strange that they were not built over the nave aisles. There is some evidence, however, that aisle vaults were initially intended, because at the east end of the south aisle there are traces of what looks like the cut-back edge of a vault around the head of the window; at the same point, it also seems that the responds (half-piers) at the east end of the arcade have been increased in height and additional shafts added (30). All of this suggests that a decision was taken to increase the height of the nave arcades but, rather than increase the height of the outer walls of the aisles at the same time in order to support vaulting at the heightened level, it was decided simply to dispense with vaulting over the aisles and keep the outer walls to the height already started.

29 The interior of the chapter house range at Dunblane Cathedral.

30 The east end of the south aisle at Dunblane Cathedral. Around the head of the window at the east end of the aisle (on the left) is what appears to be the ghost of a vault.

If this interpretation is correct, it may be wondered if a three-storeyed design, like that of Glasgow's choir (see 23),was originally intended for the central space of Dunblane's nave before the arcades were heightened, rather than the two-storeyed design we now see (31). However, whatever the original design, it should be remembered that at this period there was a growing interest in developing sophisticated two-storeyed designs. We have already seen that Elgin's nave was designed to have two storeys, and we have also considered a later attempt to reduce the impact of the triforium in the nave of Glasgow. In the course of the thirteenth century much thought was given to devising such designs, and the revised design of Dunblane played an important part in this line of thought. This was a development found elsewhere in Britain, and analogies for Dunblane can be

found in buildings such as the transepts of Hedon in Yorkshire.

In the earliest parts of the nave clearstorey as eventually built at Dunblane, at its eastern end, the windows are simple arched openings, two to each bay (see 4, 28), and there is a continuous arcade of handsomely moulded corresponding arches on the inner face of the wall passage (see 31). However, yet another innovation was soon to be made when tracery was introduced into both the windows and the inner arches. This tracery was a slightly hybrid variant on bar tracery of the type that we have seen in the transepts of Glasgow Cathedral, but in which the central opening between the arch heads is cut through a circular plate of stone and thus harks back to earlier plate tracery. Similar tracery was used in the three great windows in the west wall of the cathedral which rise above the processional entrance doorway and its flanking blind arches (32 and **colour plate 6**). On the basis of this tracery, and on analogy with the work at Glasgow, we can probably assume that Dunblane's nave was nearing completion around the 1270s.

The choir at Dunblane may initially have been intended to be less lofty than eventually built, because two arched openings in the east wall of the nave, above the chancel arch, were possibly first designed as glazed windows, though they now open into the choir (see 31). Apart from the basic shell of the eastern limb, there is relatively little in its fabric that still dates from the thirteenth century. In particular, the tracery of the windows in the south and east walls is almost entirely nineteenth century, though the great size of the window openings is original, and reflects a vogue in the later thirteenth century for windows stretching to the full extent of the available space (33 and see 70). The presbytery area at the far east end is

31 The interior of the nave of Dunblane Cathedral, with the choir beyond. The paired openings over the chancel arch may originally have been intended to be windows rather than openings into the choir.

32 The west front of Dunblane Cathedral.

particularly impressive, with light flooding in through windows on three sides.

By European standards Dunblane was not a large cathedral, though its architectural details reveal the creativity of a sequence of designing masons of high calibre, who were able to produce satisfying architecture within the constraints of a limited budget. The relatively simple solutions found for the complex planning needs of a cathedral like Dunblane were paralleled at several other cathedrals. In particular, the elongated aisle-less choir as the setting of the services of the secular canons had been foreshadowed at Brechin and to a lesser extent in the first work at Elgin; it was also to be adopted at Dunkeld and Fortrose (see **80**,

33 The choir of Dunblane Cathedral from the south-east (compare with **70**).

34 The interior of the chapter house range at Fortrose Cathedral.

83). At the latter, there was a further similarity with Dunblane in the provision of a two-storeyed elongated chapter house and sacristy range on the north side of the choir (34 and see 50). Although greatly altered on a number of occasions, with its ribbed vaulting over the lower storey and arched recesses as the seating for the chapter of canons, this range is the only part of thirteenth-century Fortrose to survive in identifiable form.

At Dunkeld, Abbot Alexander Myln of Cambuskenneth, the cathedral's historian, claimed the choir was built by Bishop William Sinclair (1309–37) (35 and see 80); however, there can be little doubt that it is largely of the mid- and later-thirteenth century, although many of the details were reconstructed in a restoration of 1814–15 by Archibald Elliot. It is five wide bays in length, with windows even larger than those of Dunblane, and its lower internal walls were enriched by decorative arcading with excellent stiff-leaf foliage, a considerable extent of which still survives along the north side. At the risk of trying to force the ecclesiastical and architectural history of the cathedral to coincide too closely, it may not be fanciful to suspect that the decision to rebuild

35 Dunkeld Cathedral from the south, with the choir to the right and the nave to the left.

the choir was taken in the time of Bishop Geoffrey de Liberatione (1236–49), during whose episcopate it was also decided to adopt the Use of Salisbury as the basis for the form of the services.

The continuing work at Kirkwall and St Andrews Cathedrals

While all of these major new campaigns were being started, work was also continuing on a number of projects begun in the twelfth century, among which were those at Kirkwall and St Andrews. At Kirkwall, despite the modifications introduced in the transept and crossing area, the continuing work inside the nave adhered remarkably closely to the scheme established about 1137, with only relatively minor changes of detail to indicate the later date (see 8). However, a rather different approach was taken when the decision was made in the early thirteenth century to extend the eastern limb by

three additional bays (36, and see 87 and colour plate 4). The reasons for doing this were probably similar to those which led to the rebuilding of the eastern limb at Glasgow, with the extended limb presumably giving space for a feretory (shrine) chapel at the east end (for St Magnus in this case) as well as for an enlarged presbytery around the high altar, while the canons' choir could now be accommodated completely within the area occupied by the original eastern limb. As elsewhere, this enlargement may have been at least partly in response to the achievement of a properly organized body of secular canons as the cathedral's chapter, and at Kirkwall the first indications of the existence of this chapter were at the election of Bishop Henry in 1247, though it must have been taking shape for some years before then.

The design of the eastward extension at Kirkwall took its lead from the earlier parts in the height and proportions of the round arched openings of the arcade and gallery stages. However, as was appropriate for areas that were liturgically more important, the piers carrying the arcades are more complex than the cylindrical piers elsewhere in the church (37); they were designed as variants on the stepped profile with engaged shafts formula that was becoming common in the earlier thirteenth century, though with shafts on the diagonal axes that were unusual in being paired and connected by a curved hollow. The capitals were decorated with a variety of foliage, including both crockets and stiff-leaf. But the greatest indications of the importance of the new eastern limb were the large window that was placed in the end wall, and the decision eventually taken to construct stone vaulting over its high central space as well as its aisles. The east window has been heavily restored and we cannot vouch for its details, though its basic forms seem to be authentic (see **36** and **colour plate 4**). Its four lights are

grouped into two pairs, and above it, occupying the full width of the window, is a twelve-petal rose, with plate tracery piercings around its edge; by any standards this was an extremely impressive window.

The decision to add high vaulting over both the eastward extension and the original part of the eastern limb is an even more extraordinary pointer to the effort being put into the cathedral of the Northern Isles, since the only other cathedral to have high vaulting over its eastern limb was St Andrews, where it was perhaps part of the effort of its bishops to demonstrate their claims to be leaders of the Scottish Church. The heightening of the walls necessitated by this decision at Kirkwall is evident externally in a

36 The choir and north transept of Kirkwall Cathedral from the north-east.

37 Stiff-leaf foliage on one of the arcade capitals of the eastern extension of Kirkwall Cathedral.

change in the colour of the masonry of the clearstorey walls (see **colour plate 4**). Once this decision had been taken for the eastern limb, it was eventually decided that the nave should also have high vaulting, and this was presumably a contributor to the fact that the cathedral remained unfinished at the Reformation. However, in the earlier thirteenth century the ambitions of Kirkwall's bishops knew no bounds, as is also made clear in the new west front started around this time.

The focal point of this new west front was a triplet of doorways (**38**), reflecting the accepted form of frontispiece to major churches elsewhere in Britain and Europe, though there is no evidence of anything comparable being planned within mainland Scotland. The two side doorways at Kirkwall were given elaborately moulded arches carried on three free-standing shafts to each jamb (flank), but the central doorway was of an altogether greater order of magnitude, with three major and four minor free-standing shafts to the jambs of the door itself, and others shafts around the small buttresses framing the doorway. It seems that some of the shafts were to be hollowed and fretted, and there may also have been plans for superstructure of some kind above the central doorway. As might be expected, the capitals of the doorways are decorated with foliage carving.

At St Andrews, so little survives of the work carried out during the thirteenth century, apart from the outer wall of the south aisle and part of the west front, that it is rather difficult to be certain of what was done (see **89**). As usual with major buildings, it seems likely that a section of the nave had been built along with the eastern limb in order to abut the lowest stage of the central tower and, also as usual, it is likely the work on the nave was stepped downwards towards the west so that the earliest upper parts of the nave to be built were themselves adequately buttressed pending the continuation of work. However, all we can now be certain of is that the lowest courses of the south aisle's wall were laid out for much of its length, but that only four bays of the windows in the upper part of this wall were built at first. In the later parts of the wall, much larger two-light aisle windows were introduced (**39**), and we can also see several changes in the ways the aisle vault was supported. At some stage in the nave building the relative proportions of the three storeys of the main space were modified, with the middle storey, the triforium, being reduced

in height from what it had been in the eastern limb. We can also see that by the west end of the nave the arcade piers had been subtly changed: they still seem to have been clusters of eight shafts, but in the nave it was the diagonal shafts that were keeled (pointed), whereas in the choir it had been the major shafts.

This very slight evidence for the internal design of the nave comes from the inside of the west front, which also shows that the high spaces of the nave were unvaulted. However, we have to be careful how we interpret this evidence, because the west front is not the original. Just as work on the cathedral was approaching its final stages, more than a hundred years after construction had been started, the nearly complete west front had to be rebuilt in the time

38 The west doorways of Kirkwall Cathedral.

39 The change of window types in the south aisle at St Andrews Cathedral.

of Bishop William Wishart (1271–9), after it was blown down in a storm. (Could this have been the same storm which damaged Arbroath Abbey in 1272?) After this the decision was taken to shorten the nave, probably by two bays, and a new west front was started on that contracted line, with a low vaulted porch being constructed across the new front within the area originally to have been occupied by the west bays of the nave (see **45**). Much of the west front had to be again reconstructed over a century later, after a fire in 1378, and the main survivor of the post-1272 campaign is the much-weathered central processional doorway, to either side of which can be seen the outline of the vaulting which once covered the porch.

The later thirteenth-century work at Elgin Cathedral

Possibly the last major cathedral building campaign to be instigated before the century closed with the outbreak of the long wars with England was at Elgin. There, the first of two major fires that punctuated the building history of the cathedral is recorded in the *Scotichronicon* for 1270, though by that point work may not yet have been completed since the start of operations in 1224. As so often, disaster was taken as the starting-point for much more than simple repairs, and the decision was taken greatly to enlarge the cathedral (see **82** and **colour plate 7**). The choir was evidently almost doubled in length, aisles were added along all but its easternmost bays and a clearstorey was added. Uniquely in a Scottish cathedral, as part of this work the nave had outer chapel aisles added along each side, incorporating the chapel already extending along the three eastern bays of the south aisle. Greater prominence was given to the main entrances into the nave, with a large processional doorway formed in the west front between the two towers (**40**), and a porch built against the lay entrance in the west bay of the south aisle. At the same time, stone vaults were added over all the aisles. Another addition was an octagonal chapter house off the north side of the choir, as the meeting room of the secular canons.

The best-preserved part of the work started after 1270 is at the east end where we see that, in keeping with the earlier work in the nave, an elegant two-storeyed design was devised, with two or three lancet windows to each bay of the clearstorey, and corresponding arches on the inner face of the mural passage. The vista down the church culminated in two tiers of five tightly packed lancets in the east gable (41). In its final late medieval form the choir was to be covered by a timber ceiling of arched profile, and there may have been a similar ceiling after 1270. Within the arch formed by the ceiling against the east gable, by the later Middle Ages there was a rose window, and this could also be a reflection of what was planned in the 1270s. In its two-storeyed design to the main spaces and tightly packed groupings of lancets in the east wall, Elgin's choir displays some similarities with English churches, such as the choir of Southwell Minster, which had been started in 1234. But it shows itself to be in step with more recent ideas in the circlets of bar tracery that were introduced at the heads of the lower windows around the site of the high altar.

The octagonal chapter house is one of only three in Scotland (see **52** and **colour plate 7**), the others being at Inchcolm and Holyrood Abbeys. Chapter houses of centralized plan were an English fashion, and again we are reminded that the exchange of architectural ideas between Scotland and England continued to be very close, though this was to end soon. The chapter house originally had windows stretching the full width of the space between the buttresses at its angles, the outlines of which are still to be seen around the later windows. The vault which now covers it internally is a late insertion, but the

40 The west doorway of Elgin Cathedral.

41 The interior of the choir of Elgin Cathedral (Billings, *The baronial and ecclesiastical antiquities of Scotland*, 1845–52).

original vault may also have rested on a central pier. The best-preserved vaults from this phase of works are over the choir aisles, where they are of the type known as tierceron, that is with additional ribs to the basic diagonally crossed pattern; yet again, this was a fashion of English origin, though Scotland was to continue using such vaults for the rest of the Middle Ages.

In the nave, the addition of outer aisles was a most unusual feature. Although double aisles were not uncommon in continental Europe, one of the few roughly contemporary parallels for this arrangement in Britain was at Chichester Cathedral, where outer aisles were being added to the nave around the second and third quarters of the century. In Scotland the closest reflection was to be at Melrose Abbey, where an outer rank of chapels was eventually added along the south flank of the nave in the fifteenth and sixteenth centuries. The eastern bays of Elgin's nave appear to have been extensively rebuilt as part of this campaign, though little remains apart from some arcade pier fragments. The finest surviving feature of this period in the nave is the west doorway which, like the west doorway of Jedburgh Abbey of a century earlier, is surmounted by three small gablets (see **40**). At a period when magnificent doorways were relatively common, Elgin's is outstanding for having eight orders of engaged shafts and arches; in a later operation, following a fire in 1390, the door was subdivided by two arched openings on its inner plane, though this may have been a replacement of what was there already.

3
The later Middle Ages

The earlier fourteenth century

In marked contrast with the ferment of cathedral-building activity in the thirteenth century, for the first three-quarters of the fourteenth century it is difficult to find evidence of more than sporadic activity. The main cause of this fall-off was the warfare that broke out with England in 1296. King Edward I of England had been called in to adjudicate on the royal succession following the death of Alexander III in 1286, and his eventual decision in favour of John Balliol was followed by the outbreak of hostilities when John and the Scots proved to be less pliable than Edward expected. Warfare continued with varying degrees of intensity for many decades to come; despite this, those cathedral-building operations that were not yet complete presumably had to be continued into the fourteenth century so far as circumstances would allow. As already said, the Bishop of Glasgow was accused of using timbers provided for his cathedral to build siege engines in 1306. In a similar spirit, at St Andrews in 1304 Edward I had taken lead from the priory roofs to provide ammunition for his engines at the siege of Stirling Castle. Nevertheless, the cathedral started at St Andrews in the 1160s was eventually ready for dedication in the presence of the great of the kingdom on 5 July 1318. Building operations within the precinct of St Andrews's cathedral priory continued after that date on some of the conventual buildings, and a spacious new rectangular chapter house,

of which fragments remain, was complete enough for Prior John of Forfar to be buried there in 1321, while work on other buildings round the cloister continued over the following decades.

Apart from these, we have only scant references to work on the cathedrals around this time. Abbot Alexander Myln said that Bishop William Sinclair started to rebuild the choir of Dunkeld in the sixth year of his episcopate, that is in 1318 (see **35**). However, as we have seen above, it is clearly earlier, and the only feature which might date from this period is the sedilia (ceremonial seats) in the south wall of the presbytery area. Another cathedral historian, Hector Boece, writing in 1522, said that rebuilding of the choir of Aberdeen was carried out by Bishop Henry Cheyne (1282–1328), who was apparently ordered to do this by Robert I to prevent him from spending the money on other things. But we cannot verify this, because nothing remains of either the eastern limb or the one that later replaced it. One other cathedral for which an early fourteenth-century date has been suggested is Lismore (**42**). This was a diminutive rectangular structure with a block for a chapter house and sacristy on its north side and a small western tower; of this only the buttressed choir now stands, albeit in a much-restored state.

As well as the difficulties of the troubled times, it is possible the cathedrals were coming to be regarded by some layfolk as less deserving

42 The choir of Lismore Cathedral from the south-west (Crown Copyright: Royal Commission on the Ancient and Historical Monuments of Scotland).

of their financial support. In the later Middle Ages there was a feeling in certain quarters that the great ecclesiastical institutions – the religious houses and cathedrals – were no longer entirely fulfilling the role that had been intended for them. So far as the cathedrals were concerned, large numbers of parishes were being impoverished to support communities of well-paid canons, some of whom were remarkable neither for their humble piety nor for their slavish attendance to duty. While depth of religious conviction was as strong – possibly even stronger – than ever, many layfolk now preferred to direct gifts they wished to offer to the church towards the places where they themselves worshipped, and where they would eventually be buried and have prayers offered for their souls. This is one reason why we find many parish churches being wholly or partly rebuilt on a more expansive scale in the later

Middle Ages, and why collegiate churches were being founded by several of the great landholding families, within which groups of clergy were intended to pray for their souls for all time to come.

Nevertheless, this shift of interest should not be over-stressed, because in Scotland most of the cathedrals were themselves parish churches, and many of the great people of the kingdom would always wish to be buried in or near the most important church in their part of the kingdom. In any case, by this time the cathedrals were already so well endowed that they were at least partly cushioned from shifting loyalties. Indeed, when cathedral building once more began to gather momentum in the later fourteenth century, and especially from the last quarter of the century, it was as if a head of pent-up energy was released, and there is little sense that there was a lack of money. Among the most significant campaigns to be started were major works necessitated by structural disasters at St Andrews, Glasgow and Elgin, while smaller-scale additions were made to Brechin and Fortrose. But the most important late medieval cathedral building operations were to be at Aberdeen and Dunkeld, where the naves were rebuilt on an ambitious scale, apparently for no more urgent reason than that finer buildings were required.

The development of new architectural ideas

A particularly fascinating aspect of the wave of cathedral building that started in the later fourteenth century is the way that most of the master masons seem to have sought ideas from places other than England. Up to this time, as we have seen in earlier chapters, architectural developments in at least the Lowland areas of Scotland had tended to run in parallel with what was happening south of the Border. After three-quarters of a century of frequently bitter warfare, however, this close architectural relationship with England was largely abandoned. There were exceptions, as when in 1372 an English mason was invited to make the tomb of David II; nevertheless, not only had England become the established enemy, but Scottish masons and their patrons had probably quite simply lost touch with architectural developments in the neighbouring country, and had little motivation to re-establish contact.

Apart from the first phase of rebuilding at Melrose Abbey, which had been destroyed by English forces in 1385 and where rebuilding was started with the support of the English king, what we see increasingly at the major Scottish buildings is a search for new architectural stimuli from further afield. Scotland was never again during the Middle Ages to adopt almost wholesale an architectural vocabulary from elsewhere, as it had in the early twelfth century;

nevertheless, individual ideas that caught the imagination of masons or patrons on continental Europe seem to have been borrowed, adapted to meet Scottish tastes and blended in with an established stock of ideas. Even when foreign masons were brought into the country to carry out work, as seems to have happened on a number of occasions, their scope for independent action was evidently limited by the need to respond to local tastes. The result of all of this was the emergence of an approach to design which, over the next one and a half centuries, produced buildings that are arguably more distinctively Scottish in character – inasmuch as they are different from anything elsewhere – than at any other time in our history. Nevertheless, it has to be stressed that there is much about the architecture of this period that we do not understand and, beyond the known facts, we must often resort to speculation.

Aberdeen Cathedral and later works at St Andrews and Brechin Cathedrals

Among the first projects to be started at this period was the rebuilding of Aberdeen Cathedral, and much of the process was recorded by Principal Hector Boece of King's College in his account of the lives of its bishops. The second bishop to bear the name Alexander Kininmund (1355–80) started rebuilding the nave, probably towards the end of his episcopate, and he raised its walls and those of the west towers by about 2.75m (9ft). Bishop Henry Lichton (1422–40) finished the walls of the nave and west towers and built the north transept, but left the central tower incomplete. His successor, Ingram Lindsay (1441–58), roofed and paved the nave, and Bishop Thomas Spens (1457–80) provided many fine furnishings. Bishop William Elphinstone (1483–1514) completed the central tower, which he ordered to be based on that of the burgh church in Perth, and started to build a larger choir. From sources other than Boece we know that many finishing touches were applied by Bishop Gavin Dunbar

1 Brechin Cathedral
from the air.

2 A painted stone from
Glasgow Cathedral, which
probably formed part of the
continuing work on the
building dedicated by Bishop
John in 1136.

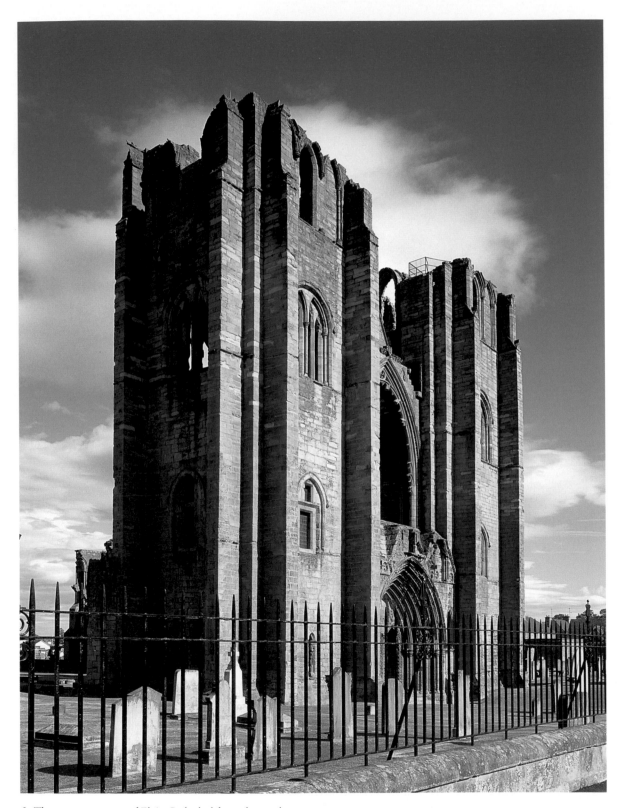

3 The western towers of Elgin Cathedral from the north-west.

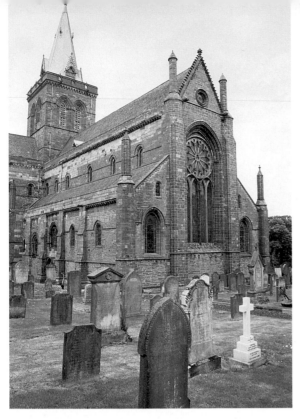

4 The choir of Kirkwall Cathedral from the south-east.

5 A reconstruction sketch of the interior of the choir of Glasgow Cathedral as it may have appeared by the later Middle Ages. The masonry and the timber ceiling would have been lime-washed, and the more important parts then richly decorated, while the other walls were perhaps painted with lines in imitation of masonry jointing (David Simon).

6 The nave and tower of Dunblane Cathedral seen from the
Allan Water to the south-west.

7 The east gable of the choir and the chapter house of Elgin Cathedral.

8 The south aisle and chapel of Fortrose Cathedral from the south (the clock tower is a later addition).

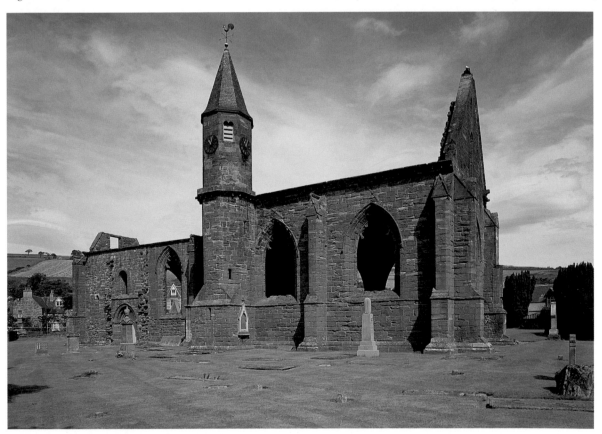

9 The nave of Whithorn Cathedral from the south-west.

10 The entrance front of the archbishop's castle at
St Andrews as remodelled for Archbishop Hamilton in
the mid-sixteenth century.

11 The tower-house of the castle of the bishop of Moray at Spynie.

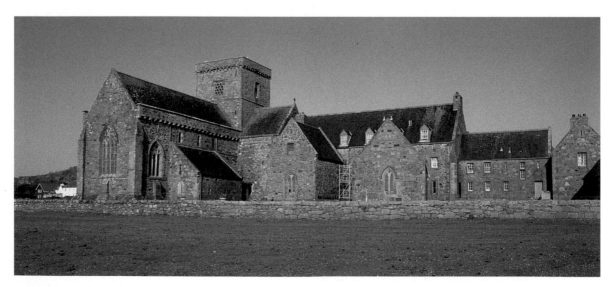

12 The restored abbey church and conventual buildings of Iona from the north-east.

(1518–32), who completed the south transept, which was his own burial place, to the designs of the mason Thomas French, and built the spires on the western towers. He also placed the ribbed heraldic ceiling over the nave, which is decorated with the arms of the leaders of the Scottish Church under the leadership of the papacy, the Scottish aristocracy under the leadership of the king and the monarchs of Christendom headed by the Holy Roman Emperor. This ceiling is recorded as the work of a wright named as James Winter, though it might be that this is a distortion of the name of John Fendour, the wright who worked on the cathedral's central tower, as well as at St Nicholas's Parish Church and possibly at King's College Chapel in Aberdeen.

Only the nave, with its south porch and two western towers, together with the lower walls of the transepts, now survive, and these are austerely imposing works hewn mainly from the intractable local granite (43). The western towers are particularly impressive tower-house-like structures; between them is a processional doorway surmounted by a west window in the form of seven narrow equal-height openings. Internally the nave is a two-storeyed design, though there is incomplete correspondence between the segmentally arched openings on to the clearstorey passage and the arcade of arches which supports it (44). A striking feature of the nave is the use of heavy cylindrical piers, since such piers had been out of fashion for major churches in both Scotland and England for many years.

These piers could be one of our first pointers to a willingness on the part of Scottish patrons and masons to look directly to the continent for new ideas. Cylindrical piers were again to become fashionable once more in many countries (except in England), but nowhere was this the case so early and to so great an extent as in the Netherlands, where such piers had been designed for the new choir of St Rombout's Church in Mechelen, begun in 1342. It was with the Netherlands that Scotland enjoyed its closest

43 The towers, nave and porch of Aberdeen Cathedral from the south-west (Billings, *The baronial and ecclesiastical antiquities of Scotland*, 1845–52).

commercial links, and the arts of that area became increasingly influential, so it would not be surprising if it were from there that the idea of the piers was taken. It is perhaps also worth mentioning that the predecessor of the bishop who started building the nave, Bishop John Rait, earlier may have been a canon of one of the churches in Bruges, the city through which most Scottish trade with the Netherlands was directed. But the strongest pointer to Netherlandish inspiration at Aberdeen is the design of the freestone piers at the east end of the nave, which were apparently the first to be built, and which supported the west side of the central tower. These piers, which have a massive cylindrical core and almost equally massive half columns towards the four principal directions, are of a type seldom found outside the Netherlands.

But the Netherlands were not to be the only source of fresh ideas in Scotland, and at St Andrews it seems inspiration may also have

44 The interior of the nave of Aberdeen Cathedral (Crown Copyright: Royal Commission on the Ancient and Historical Monuments of Scotland).

been sought from France. In this connection it should be remembered that, although Scotland's strongest commercial links were with the Netherlands, the nation's closest political ties were with France, the country with which there had been a long succession of mutual aid treaties, the first of real importance being as early as 1295. St Andrews suffered a devastating fire in 1378, which necessitated much rebuilding, and the problem was made worse when the south transept gable collapsed in 1409. Work dragged on for many years and, though little of it survives, it seems several masons were involved. The most prominent feature is the large window cut through the upper parts of the east wall by Prior James Haldenstone (1418–43) towards the end of the rebuilding (see **10**). In the south wall of the south transept, however, there are the lower

courses of a cylindrical half-pier; this was presumably part of an arcade of cylindrical piers built after the collapse of this wall in 1409 and, like the piers at Aberdeen, it could be a sign of Netherlandish inspiration on this part of the design. But in an earlier part of the rebuilding, in the nave, it seems other influences were at work. The only parts of the rebuilt nave arcade piers to survive are the lowest sections of a number of bases, and the way these are elongated towards the central space suggests there was a carefully devised subdivision into bays by shafts rising through the piers and up the higher parts of the walls, in a way that was more common on the continent of Europe than in Britain.

Slightly more informative than the arcade sub-bases is one of the windows in the rebuilt wall above the great west doorway, which evidently had tracery consisting of triplets of

45 The west front of St Andrews Cathedral from the north-west.

46 A displaced corbel at Glasgow Cathedral which may have been carved for the mason John Morow.

circlets (45). Windows of this type had first emerged in France around the 1230s, and had then been taken up widely in other countries, including England. However, while they had then passed out of use in England, they had remained fashionable rather longer in France; it is also worth mentioning that the windows at St Andrews are stilted (vertically extended at the head) in a way that is particularly common in France. Bearing in mind that the two bishops who are the most likely patrons of this part of the work had strong French connections (William Landallis was elected bishop with the support of the French king and Walter Traill had been a student at two French universities), a French inspiration for the window cannot be unlikely. Beyond this, we know there was a French mason at St Andrews around this time. This is because the mason of the second phase of works at Melrose Abbey, John Morow, left an inscription there saying that he was of Parisian birth and recording some of the other buildings on which he had worked, of which one was St Andrews. It must be said that from what we can understand of Morow's approach to design at Melrose and other works that he listed, of which parts of Paisley Abbey and Lincluden Collegiate Church are the most important to survive, it is unlikely that anything still visible in the nave of St Andrews was designed by Morow himself. However, it seems reasonable to suspect he was there with a team

of other French craftsmen, and that it is the work of some of his colleagues we see in the nave.

In his Melrose inscription, Morow also stated that he had worked at Glasgow, and the evidence for his work there may survive in a pair of displaced corbels (projecting stone blocks) carved with prophets carrying scrolls on which their prophecies would have been painted (46). Such prophet corbels were common in much of Europe, but the only places where we know of them in Scotland are Glasgow, Melrose and Lincluden, all of which are included on Morow's list at Melrose, and so it seems all of them could have been carved under his guidance. It is not certain where these corbels were used at Glasgow, though it is thought they are from the southern of the two towers of the west front, which was demolished in 1846.

Among the pointers to growing continental influence in Scotland are the designs of a number of windows. Around the turn of the thirteenth and fourteenth centuries English masons had developed types of tracery using the ogee (double curve), and the delightfully fluid designs that resulted are usually described as curvilinear or decorated. However, a divergence then took place; whereas in England such designs were increasingly rejected in the second half of the fourteenth century in favour of designs in which grid-like rectilinear patterns predominated, within many countries of continental Europe curvilinear designs were taken up and further developed. In Scotland we find curvilinear designs from around the early fifteenth century and, since it seems most unlikely that they would have been reflecting an abandoned English fashion, it is probable they were inspired by contemporary fashions on the continent.

Within a cathedral context a fine example of such curvilinear tracery is the window inserted in the west front at Brechin (see 2). Two separate building campaigns were in progress at Brechin from the later fourteenth century, with work on the north-western tower apparently having been restarted in a workmanlike fashion by Bishop Patrick Leuchars (1351–*c.* 1383). But the charming complexities of the west window are in a different spirit from the tower, and the closest Scottish parallel for it is a window on the north side of the presbytery at Melrose Abbey, which was presumably designed by one of Morow's masons. It seems at least a possibility – if no more than that – that the guiding spirit behind the choice of such a design at Brechin could have been Bishop Walter Forrester (1407–25), who had been a student at Paris between 1375 and 1398, and who would therefore have been well placed to appreciate the ideas being introduced into Scotland by Morow and his fellows.

The nave of Dunkeld Cathedral

Although, as we have seen above, it is likely Abbot Alexander Myln was mistaken in supposing that Bishop William Sinclair had built the choir of Dunkeld, he was on surer ground in talking about more recent works. He had been dean of the Angus division of the diocese between 1505 and 1514, was official of the whole diocese until he became abbot of Cambuskenneth in 1519 and was thus well placed to know. He records that the nave was started by Bishop Robert Cardeny in 1406, and that it was completed and dedicated by Bishop Thomas Lauder in 1464 (**47**). Lauder went on to add a porch on the south side of the nave, and on the north side of the choir he started a square two-storeyed chapter house and sacristy in 1457. Lauder's most important addition was the tower at the north-west corner of the nave, which he started in 1469, and which was finished by his successor, Bishop James Livingston. Linked with this addition was the insertion of an exquisite window in the west wall of the nave.

47 The nave of Dunkeld Cathedral from the south-east.

48 The interior of the nave of Dunkeld Cathedral looking west.

The design of Dunkeld's nave is a particularly valuable pointer to Scottish tastes at this time (**48** and see **80**). The central space is three storeys high, with cylindrical arcade piers, subdivided round arches at triforium level, and a clearstorey which is without a passage, presumably because the walls are relatively thin. The south aisle was intended to be covered with stone vaults, though metal pins projecting from the vault springings suggest they were completed in timber, and certainly the north aisle appears to have had fully timber vaults. The central space was also timber-covered. The cylindrical piers and round arches are sometimes regarded as a sign of a revival of twelfth-century ideas, and it is true that in a number of late medieval churches we do find a renewed interest in earlier types of design. But at Dunkeld the pier bases and capitals are in the most recent fashion, and the round triforium (middle storey) arches also reflect a revival of such arches elsewhere in Europe. On balance it again seems more likely that we are seeing the influence of Netherlandish architectural ideas, as at Aberdeen (see **44**) and in the south transept at St Andrews. An awareness of current European fashions is similarly apparent in the aisle windows, with their curvilinear tracery, especially in the two larger easternmost windows of each aisle, which lit the chapels at these points.

Of the window inserted secondarily in Dunkeld's west front, only the tracery stumps remain, but from this we can see that it was very similar to a window in the south transeptal chapel at St Michael's Church in Linlithgow (**49**). The main motif of both these windows was an enormous triangle with curved sides at the arch head, which contained three circlets and three vesica (almond) shapes, within each of which were subsidiary interlocking tracery forms. It may be significant that tracery of this sort has some parallels in south-eastern France,

because it is possible that a French mason was responsible for the window at Linlithgow. We know that a mason named John French was buried in the church in 1489, and may have been involved in part of its building; in view of the details of this window is it possible that his name indicated his national origins? (The Thomas French who worked on the transepts at Aberdeen was a later member of the same family, which may suggest they had by then settled in Scotland.) If a mason of French origin did indeed design the Linlithgow window, was he additionally responsible for the closely similar window at Dunkeld? The adjacent tower at Dunkeld also has a smaller window with good curvilinear tracery at its base, though the tower as a whole is essentially a rather less

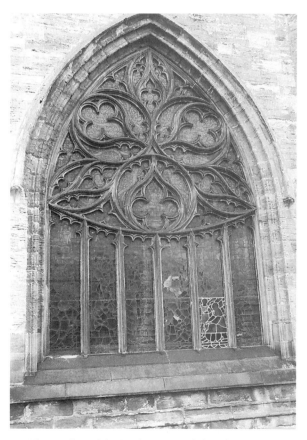

49 The window of the south transeptal chapel at Linlithgow St Michael; the west window of Dunkeld would have been very like this, apart from differences at the heads of the lower lights.

original design, and the case for a French designer for this part is less strong. Its position and relationship with the cathedral nave, incidentally, recall the tower at Brechin and also the one at Glasgow before the second west tower was added (see **2, 27**).

Later works at Elgin, Fortrose and Glasgow Cathedrals

At Elgin extensive rebuilding was necessary after Alexander, Earl of Buchan, a son of King Robert II who came to be known as the Wolf of Badenoch, set fire to the cathedral in 1390. Further damage was caused when a son of the Lord of the Isles attacked it in 1402, and rebuilding occupied much of the later Middle Ages. The first phase of repairs was probably at the east end, so that the cathedral could again be used for services, and those parts were probably complete before the death of Bishop John Innes in 1414, since he is said to have started reconstruction of the central tower. (Unfortunately it seems to have fallen down again afterwards.) Work had progressed as far

as the west front of the nave by the time of Bishop Columba Dunbar (1422–35), because his arms are above the west window. There was then a long pause before the chapter house was repaired, since its central pier bears the arms of Bishop Andrew Stewart (1482–1501) (see **52**), and the tower was again rebuilt in 1506. In the earlier phases of rebuilding great efforts were made to ensure that the new work was in sympathy with what was already there. The vaulting of the aisles was carefully repaired, with some new bosses being inserted, and large windows were inserted in their walls, which took a lead from the smaller windows of the 1270s in their combinations of arcs and circlets.

This phase of work at Elgin was an influence on additions made on the south side of Fortrose Cathedral, where a chapel, aisle and porch were built, possibly incorporating parts of an earlier aisle (**50, 51**, and see **83**; **colour plate 8**). The patroness of this work is thought to have been

50 The south aisle and chapel of Fortrose Cathedral from the north-west. The chapter house range is on the left.

Euphemia, Countess of Ross in her own right, who was – ironically enough – the wife of the Earl of Buchan who burnt Elgin Cathedral, though she clearly had little sympathy with the less endearing side of her husband's nature. The countess had been married first to Walter Leslie, and the arms of Leslie are displayed on the vaulting of the addition, though the presence of the arms of Bishop John Bullock (1418–39) suggest the aisle was finished only after her own death in 1395. The chapel was broader than the aisle to its west and, since a tomb was designed as an integral part of its eastern arch, it was probably intended as a chantry chapel, perhaps for the countess's first husband who had died in 1382. The similarities between these additions to Fortrose and the earlier phase of rebuilding at Elgin are so close that it is possible a number of the same masons were involved in both. This is seen particularly in the window tracery, some of which had intersecting arcs containing small circlets. It should be noted, however, that it was not just the most recent features of Elgin that were followed. The tierceron vaulting, and the design of the buttresses – which have broad chamfers to their upper sections and which are capped by small gablets – are closely related to details of the 1270s at Elgin.

Later works at Elgin showed rather less concern to take their lead from what was already there than was seen in the earlier stages. Along the outer chapel aisles of the nave, lateral gables were constructed around the heads of large windows (see **16**), though even here the cornice details, with their small intersecting arches, may have been copied from thirteenth-century work. The saw-tooth appearance of these gables may reflect a fashion that had re-emerged in the Low Countries at this time. The remodelled west front of the nave, between the two towers and above the doorway, was almost entirely given over to a vast traceried window. The way this rises up into the gable, together with the shape of masonry around the rose window in the east gable of the choir, suggests that the main spaces of the cathedral were being

51 The interior of the south chapel and aisle of Fortrose Cathedral looking west.

covered by timber ceilings of arched profile. Below the west window an inner skin was added to the back of the doorway, with two highly enriched sub-arches carried on a trumeau (central pier) (see **40**). While much of the cathedral was receiving windows that were probably larger than the originals, the chapter house was given smaller ones (**52**). This contraction of openings, together with the thickening of the upper walls internally, was presumably to afford adequate support for the new vault. The replacement windows were filled with curvilinear tracery, though it must be admitted that some of the new designs were less satisfactory than others.

Having considered the consequence of fires at St Andrews and Elgin, we must now look at the results of another, at Glasgow. We do not know exactly when this fire was, but in correspondence with the pope in 1406 it

52 The interior of the chapter house of Elgin Cathedral as rebuilt in the late fifteenth century (Billings, *The baronial and ecclesiastical antiquities of Scotland*, 1845–52).

becomes clear that the cathedral had been burnt after being hit by lightning in the time of Bishop Matthew Glendinning (1387–1408). The main areas referred to as damaged were the central tower, choir, chapter house and vestry. Accounts of damage were usually exaggerated in the hope of attracting greater sympathy, and it seems likely the damage to the masonry structure of the choir was limited, though the timber roof and furnishings could certainly have been damaged without our now knowing of it. We are also ignorant of the extent of damage to the vestry, since only the treasury which formed the lower storey of that structure now survives. However, there is no doubt that total rebuilding of the central tower and spire were called for, and there was also major rebuilding in the two-storeyed chapter house.

Reconstruction of the tower, with its single storey rising above the surrounding roofs, each face of which is pierced by four equal-height windows, was started by Bishop William Lauder (1408–26), who placed his coat of arms on the parapet (**53**). The handsome broached spire, with pinnacles at the angles and with four tiers of lucarnes (small gabled windows) was completed by Bishop John Cameron (1426–46). Cameron also started the repairs to the chapter house, since his arms are on the repaired vault of the lower storey. Work on the upper storey of the chapter house had to be more extensive, and it was Bishop William Turnbull (1447–54) who completed it and placed his arms on the parapet. At this upper level virtually the whole vault had to be replaced, and since most of the windows were rebuilt it seems that work was even more extensive than might at first appear. As with the first phase of operations at Elgin, however, there was an attempt to make the new work sit easily with the original. Accompanying all of this there may have been a reordering of the choir. In 1420 the pope's permission was sought to move St

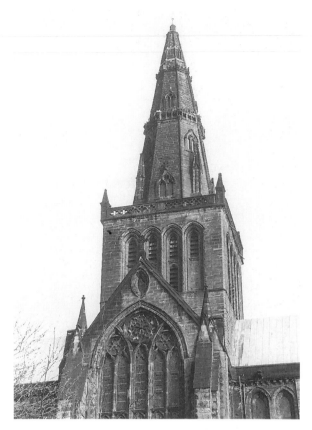

53 The central tower and spire of Glasgow Cathedral.

Kentigern's relics into a new shrine of gold and silver, and the stone screen or pulpitum, which separated the canon's choir from the rest of the church, also looks to be of around this time (**54**). Originally this screen had statues framed within the four shallow arches on each side of the central doorway, but these were removed when new altars were placed here, and it is only by close inspection that it is possible to see where their supporting corbels were cut back.

Some other cathedral building operations

Apart from the major building operations listed above, and the continuing work at Kirkwall, where the main shell (though not its vaulting) was approaching completion with the construction of the disappointing upper parts of the west front in the time of Bishop Andrew Painter (1477–*c*. 1506), there is evidence for a variety of lesser-scale works at most cathedrals.

54 The pulpitum of Glasgow Cathedral, with the later altar platforms in front of it.

There is insufficient space to list them all here, though it is probably true to say that some work was taking place at most cathedrals up to the eve of the Reformation, the main exceptions probably being Lismore and Snizort, where the location was evidently regarded as unsatisfactory.

At Glasgow, the diocese's first archbishop, Robert Blackadder (1483–1508), restarted work on the laterally projecting aisle off the south transept by constructing a vault over it, though no more than the lowest courses of its upper storey were ever built. At Dunblane, the three bishops of the Chisholm dynasty (1487–1569) raised the twelfth-century tower to a height more in scale with the rest of the building, rebuilt the choir parapet and formed a chapel in the western bays of the south aisle dedicated to the Holy Blood and St Blaise (see 28, 33). The main physical evidence for the last of these is a pair of windows of very simple design, which were presumably regarded primarily as frames for stained glass rather than as features in their own right. A chapel in a similar position, but in this case dedicated to the Virgin as the deliverer of souls from hell, was formed at Dunkeld by Bishop George Brown (1483–1515), and again it is a rebuilt window that is the main evidence for what was done.

If these lesser contributions seem relatively undemanding in scale, it should be remembered that by this time most of the dioceses already had fine cathedral buildings. But in looking at such works it should also be recollected that some of them reflect changing trends in worship throughout Europe as whole. As part of a growing concern with the sinfulness of man came a yearning to identify more closely with the suffering that Christ had undergone on behalf of mankind, and feast days were introduced which encouraged contemplation of aspects such as the blood he had shed and the wounds he had endured. At the same time many came to regard themselves as increasingly unworthy to address God directly, and saw prayers through the saints, especially through Christ's mother who had herself suffered so much, as a less audacious way of approaching the godhead. It was to meet such needs that the chapels at Dunblane and Dunkeld Cathedrals were formed, and if the chapels themselves involved relatively little major structural change, the furnishings they contained would have been quite splendid, especially in their painted imagery. Indeed, much effort and money were expended on furnishings as the setting for worship throughout the cathedrals as a whole in the later Middle Ages though, because of their association with rejected forms of worship, they suffered particularly badly at the Reformation. Some of the very limited evidence for them will be discussed more fully in the next chapter.

4
The life of the cathedrals

The cathedral clergy

Although a cathedral was primarily a bishop's church, being one of the symbols of his authority over his diocese, many people were required to ensure the maintenance of a constant round of worship within it, to administer its possessions, and – at least in principle – to elect new bishops. The more important of those people formed the cathedral's ruling body, known as the chapter.

In England, because those responsible for reorganizing the church after the Norman Conquest were themselves monks, the Anglo-Saxon practice of having monasteries attached to some cathedrals had continued. Consequently, about half of the cathedrals south of the Border were monastic throughout the Middle Ages, with communities of Benedictine monks (or of Augustinian canons regular in one case) acting as the cathedral chapters. Within Europe as a whole this was most unusual, though there was to be some reflection of the practice in Scotland. At St Andrews, Bishop Robert, who was himself an Augustinian canon, eventually succeeded in replacing the existing bodies of clergy there with canons by 1144. Similarly, there were probably Augustinian canons at Whithorn at one stage, until they were replaced by the even stricter order of Premonstratensian canons in about 1177. There were also thoughts of having Augustinian chapters elsewhere; in 1237 consideration was given to moving the cathedral of Dunblane diocese to the Augustinian abbey of Inchaffray, while canons regular had been regarded as a possible chapter at Aberdeen in 1157. As an alternative, monks had been considered at Aberdeen as well, as they may also have been at Kirkwall twenty years earlier; even as late as 1498 the idea was mooted of basing the diocese of the Isles at Iona, in which case the monks of the Benedictine abbey might have become the cathedral chapter.

Nevertheless, despite all of those cases, in most Scottish dioceses, including those that were only absorbed within the Scottish church at a later date, chapters made up of secular (that is, non-monastic) canons were generally preferred (55). With such a chapter each canon lived separately, rather than within a cloistered community, usually having his own manse in the cathedral precinct (see 62, 63), and enjoying his own income, known as a prebend. However, the difficulty in this was that adequate endowments had to be found to finance these chapters, which frequently seems to have taken some time to achieve. In several cases there is evidence that a chapter of sorts was at first made up of the senior clergy or the parish priests of the diocese or town in which the cathedral was situated. In such cases the chapter was thus essentially a synod of clergy, and its head was usually an archdeacon, the cleric responsible for the discipline of the parish clergy within his division of the diocese.

Such synodal chapters were not regarded as ideal, however, and funds were usually

55 A secular canon of a cathedral chapter. Walter Idill, Official of Aberdeen diocese (c.1446–68) from his tomb in Aberdeen Cathedral. He is wearing his mass vestments, together with the fur-lined almuce (hood) which distinguished him as a member of a cathedral chapter.

parochial clergy. Nevertheless, while the impoverishment of the parishes was certainly unfortunate, the process should be understood within the context of its time. It is in fact doubtful if it had ever been assumed that all of the teinds of all the parishes would go to the parochial clergy themselves and, especially in the later Middle Ages when the income of the Church was being adversely affected by a number of factors, including falling exports and ever higher exactions from the papacy, it was perhaps not unnatural that the cathedrals should take advantage of whatever sources of income were available to them.

eventually found to endow prebends for a chapter of secular canons. Although this was sometimes done through the provision of land, particularly in the earlier phases of establishing cathedral chapters, the most common means was by appropriating the teinds (tithes) of considerable numbers of parishes. Each canon would usually take his title from the parish that provided him with his main income, while the revenues from yet more parishes might be put into a common fund to supplement their income and to meet a variety of other needs. Glasgow eventually had thirty-two canons, while the much poorer diocese of Dornoch probably had no more than thirteen, and it is doubtful how far the diocese of the Isles ever had an effective chapter at all.

In general all of this worked well enough for the cathedrals and meant, incidentally, that at least some of the canons were very wealthy, though the system inevitably led to the impoverishment of many parishes, and possibly to declining educational standards among the

The organization of the cathedral chapters tended to be based on English examples, with the constitution of Salisbury being adapted for the chapters of Glasgow and Dunkeld, while York was also seen as a useful exemplar. Lincoln was the model copied at Elgin, largely due to the very close relations enjoyed with that diocese while Simon de Gunby was first dean and then bishop of Moray between 1230 and 1251. Leading the canons, there were usually four dignitaries: the dean (at Kirkwall known as the provost), the chanter or precentor, the chancellor and the treasurer. The dean was the head of the chapter, while the chanter was responsible for the cathedral's music and the 'sang schule'; the chancellor was the legal officer of the establishment and also had responsibility for any grammar school attached to the cathedral, while the treasurer dealt with the financial aspects of the chapter's work and cared for its more precious possessions. The archdeacons of the dioceses also often had a place in the chapter of their cathedral. During church services the dignitaries occupied the stalls at the ends of the two ranks which extended along each flank of the choir, and these were usually given greater prominence than all others apart from that of the bishop.

In a number of the wealthier cathedrals some of the dignitaries had substitutes. The dean's was the sub-dean, the chanter's was the sub-chanter or succentor and the treasurer's the sacrist. In fact, absenteeism was to be a major problem in all cathedral chapters, and even more among the canons than the dignitaries. In some cases this was because canonries had been given to a loyal servant of the crown or Church, with little assumption that the appointee would attend chapter meetings or cathedral services on a regular basis. In other cases, the holders of the office might have to be absent at university, on embassies or on other important matters. However, not all cases of absenteeism can have been explained away thus, and there were efforts to encourage more regular attendance by threatening the loss of part of the prebendal income and by sharing the common fund among only those who attended for a certain proportion of the year, as was certainly attempted at Aberdeen. To ensure that services were carried out in a seemly way most canons were obliged to provide a vicar (substitute) for themselves, who could be a priest, a deacon or a sub-deacon. These vicars had to show that they were able to memorize and sing the services, and had to give sureties for their care of the choir vestments which were usually provided for them by their canon. Strict rules were drawn up for their behaviour, and at Elgin there were even regulations covering their avoidance of taverns. Several cathedrals had choristers: Aberdeen may have had eight, though six seems to have been more usual.

Bishops did not always have an easy relationship with their cathedral chapters. The scope for difficulty was perhaps greatest where the bishop had no seat in chapter, as at Dunblane, Dunkeld, Glasgow, St Andrews, Whithorn and perhaps Lismore. At Glasgow in 1487 Bishop Robert Blackadder made a slightly undignified attempt to win a place in chapter, even offering to provide the prebend, but he was thwarted in his plan.

Technically the chapter was responsible for electing bishops, using one of three approved methods: *per scrutinium* (by a vote); *per compromissum* (the choice being given to a delegated group); and *per inspirationem* (by unanimous acclaim). However, bishops were far too important for their election to be left so loosely controlled for long, and both kings and popes considered that theirs should be the right to make the choice. Popes argued that they were the rulers of the Church and that bishops were their subordinates, while kings increasingly resented external interference within their kingdoms, especially since they relied so heavily on bishops to serve as officers of state. On balance it was probably the kings who were best able to gain their ends. As early as 1487 Innocent VIII agreed that he and his successors would delay making appointments to major ecclesiastical vacancies for eight (later increased to twelve) months to await the views of the king, during which period the king had the additional advantage of being able to enjoy the income of the vacant dioceses.

Nevertheless, there was still scope for unseemly behaviour, as when there were no fewer than six claimants for the vacant archdiocese of St Andrews, following the death in 1513 at the battle of Flodden of James IV's illegitimate son, who had been appointed archbishop in 1504 but who was still too young to have been consecrated. In this case the pope hoped to take advantage of the confusion after Flodden by providing his own nephew, Cardinal Innocenzo Cibo, to the vacancy, though it turned out that there were stronger minds in Scotland than he had expected. The approach that was eventually adopted, and that was enshrined in an act of 1526, was that the king would nominate his candidate to the pope and instruct the chapter whom they were to elect; the pope would then 'provide' the candidate and subsequently confirm the election. Soon after this, Henry VIII of England rejected the pope as head of the church there, and successive popes became even more anxious to ensure that Scotland's kings did not follow him along the path to Reformation, meaning that they were yet more willing to grant favours to faithful adherents of the Church.

In all of this it should be remembered that then, just as now, it was the unseemly aspects of

Church life that came to be reflected in the records and in the formulation of rules. For all the inequalities of the system, the medieval Church was probably in general well enough served by its bishops and cathedral chapters and, if there were relatively few outright saints amongst their ranks, there were some excellent administrators, a number of fine scholars and many enlightened patrons of the arts.

Worship in the cathedrals

There would have been few times of the day when a visitor to a medieval cathedral would not have found one or more services taking place in parts of it. Not only was a cathedral the place where the permanent body of clergy attached to it carried out its worship, but the majority of Scottish cathedrals, apart from St Andrews, Elgin and perhaps a few others, were also parish churches and thus had to meet the spiritual needs of the local communities. In addition many cathedrals were major places of pilgrimage, with relics of St Ninian at Whithorn, of St Andrew at St Andrews, of St Kentigern at Glasgow (see **22**), of St Gilbert at Dornoch and of St Columba at Dunkeld among the more significant. As the leading church of its diocese, a cathedral would also attract throngs of the faithful at the great festivals, while the wealthier parishioners, together with many of the diocese's nobility and higher clergy, might hope to be buried within or outside it. Some of those granted burial rights would establish altars and chapels in association with their tombs, at which prayers would be said for their souls (see **58**).

The most important worship in a cathedral was that which took place closest to the ceremonial area around the high altar known as the presbytery, and which was carried out by or on behalf of the canons. In the two cathedrals staffed by canons regular (St Andrews and Whithorn), this worship was like that in the monastic churches, known as the *opus dei* or work of God. The main element was a daily round of services made up of psalms, antiphons, readings and prayers, which began in the early

hours of the morning (though the precise hour depended on the time of year) and which continued until mid-evening. The names of these services were nocturns (later called matins), matins (later called lauds), prime, terce, sext, none, vespers and compline. In addition, there were probably two communal celebrations of the mass, while individual canons may have celebrated further private masses either for themselves or on behalf of others. Few layfolk would expect to have access to the canons' choir, but this would not have seemed odd, since they had their own services elsewhere. Indeed, the idea underlying the canons' services was that they were the worship of a religious community on behalf of the world, for which the world was grateful but in which it saw little need to become more closely involved.

The worship of the secular canons in the other cathedrals took its lead from the services at the monastic cathedrals. If we consider Aberdeen as an illustration of this, we know that matins and lauds began at about 5.30 a.m. in the summer months, followed by all the other services in regular succession, and with vespers and compline in the mid-evening. Ideally, the full complement of canons should have been present at all of the services, though it is clear that the main burden of the daily services usually fell on the vicars of the choir, with support from the choristers.

The liturgy as followed in Scotland was broadly the same as in the rest of western Christendom, though within this uniformity there was scope for a range of local variations. Most Scottish dioceses at first chose to follow the usages developed for the English diocese of Salisbury, known as the Sarum Rite (form of service). Apart from other more-or-less minor differences from services in the rest of Europe, there was great emphasis on the importance of music in this rite, and there were also particularly impressive ceremonies as part of the build-up to the celebration of Easter. The Sarum Rite was adopted at Glasgow by the mid-thirteenth century, and in 1242 it was decided at Elgin that it was to be the model followed 'in psalmody, in reading, in singing and in all else pertaining to worship'.

Yet the cathedral liturgy was not immune from change. The historian Hector Boece, writing in the early sixteenth century, remarked that the reign of James I (1406–37) had seen a great increase in the elaboration of services, and it seems this also led to an increased richness of the furnishings provided as the setting for them (56). However, by the time that Boece was writing there had long been a sense that inspiration should be sought from places other than England for the form of the more flexible parts of the services, and that more Scottish saints should be commemorated. The earlier stages of the growing sense of national identity came soon after the outbreak of the Wars of Independence in the 1290s, when antagonism against England was high, though the greatest developments in this direction came in the later fifteenth century. The attempt to develop a specifically Scottish usage was perhaps eventually best epitomized in the publication of the Aberdeen breviary for Bishop Elphinstone in 1510.

Those cathedrals that were centres of pilgrimage might be planned so as to allow pilgrims to pass between the various parts they wished to visit without disturbing the services of the canons. At Glasgow there were at least two, and possibly three, main foci of interest (see **22** and **colour plate 5**). In the crypt below the choir was the site of the tomb of St Kentigern, and attention was concentrated on this by a masterly architectural manipulation of the spaces. There were also relics in a feretory (shrine) behind the high altar, and pilgrims were able to reach this along the aisles on each side of the canons' choir and along a cross-aisle which interconnected the two side aisles behind the high altar. (In this there were some similarities with the final arrangement at St Andrews, where the aisles gave access to the feretory chapel at the east end, which was eventually lit by an enlarged window) (see **10**). At Glasgow there may also have been an area devoted to the holy man Fergus, whose

hearse Kentigern was believed to have followed to Glasgow. It is possible that Whithorn was similarly planned with an eye to the circulation of pilgrims, though we understand very little about the eastern parts of the cathedral there.

The main services for the layfolk, and particularly for those who used a cathedral as their parish church, were in the nave, and their principal altars were against the west side of the screens separating the nave from the canons' choir (see **56**). The nave would also contain a baptismal font, and probably a pulpit for sermons. The increased emphasis placed on preaching after the Reformation has fostered an impression that there was little preaching in the medieval church, and perhaps there was less than there should have been; indeed, many of the parochial clergy were probably insufficiently educated to be able to preach adequately. Nevertheless, preaching was always regarded as important, and the fourth Lateran Council of 1215 had urged bishops to ensure that there was more. The Dominican friars, whose order was founded in the aftermath of that Council, saw preaching as such a central element of their life that they were known as 'friars preachers', and they were probably often called upon to preach in churches other than their own. Nevertheless, some Scottish bishops were not only renowned preachers themselves, but encouraged others to preach, and we know that cathedral libraries contained books to help preachers compose their sermons.

In addition to the high altar in the presbytery, and the main nave altars against the choir screen, there would have been many other altars. Architectural provision for chapels to house some of them is still evident at many cathedrals. At Glasgow there was a row of four enclosed chapels at the east end at both choir and crypt levels (see **84, 85**); at Elgin outer aisles were added along the length of the nave aisles for additional chapels, while there are spaces at the east end of the choir aisles for others (see **82**); at St Andrews there were chapels on the east side of the two transepts and at the ends of the choir aisles (see **89**); and at Dunblane

56 A reconstruction sketch of the interior of Dunkeld
Cathedral as it may have looked in the later Middle Ages,
showing some of the furnishings that would be expected in
a major cathedral of the period (Harry Bland).

emphasis was given to chapels at the east end of the nave aisles by raised gables (see **4, 30, 79**). Many other examples of such side chapels could be cited, though the majority of lesser altars have left little architectural trace. At St Andrews, for example, records suggest there may have been more than thirty altars, and Glasgow probably had a similar number, most of which would have been tucked into small spaces within the aisles or against the arcade piers. Some of these were for the cathedral clergy to celebrate private masses, while others were associated with the cult of saints venerated at the cathedral.

However, most lesser altars were founded by individuals or for groups such as trade or religious guilds, who wished to have masses offered for their welfare in life and for their souls after death. This was to ensure their ultimate salvation and to reduce the time they might have to spend in purgatory as punishment for their sins. The fear of purgatory was very real, particularly in the later Middle Ages, and almost everyone would make some provision for prayers to be offered for their souls. The poor would perhaps pay for a small number of masses to be said at a particular altar, while the rich might hope to pay for masses to be said for all time at an altar they had specially founded for this purpose, and which might be as close to their burial place as possible. Such foundations were known as perpetual chantries, and many priests were appointed for this purpose, although in a cathedral some of the priest-vicars would add to their income by offering soul masses.

Cathedral furnishings

Taking account of all this, it is important to remember that, internally, a cathedral was not a single undivided space, since much of the interior would have been partitioned by screens into sub-spaces of varying sizes (see **56**). So far as the principal body of clergy, the canons, was concerned, although they would process through other parts of the building, during most

of their corporate services they were within the choir. This usually occupied two or three bays to the west of the presbytery and was enclosed by walls or screens. In the earlier cathedrals (except perhaps at St Andrews) the canons' choir probably extended down from the eastern limb into the eastern parts of the nave, though in cathedrals rebuilt from the thirteenth century onwards there was a preference for the choir to be entirely contained within an extended eastern limb. This meant there was a clearer architectural distinction between the part of the building occupied by the canons and the part used by layfolk.

Within the canons' choir would be one or two rows of wooden stalls extending down each of its sides; if it was an aisle-less structure these stalls were probably set against the side walls, while in aisled structures they were against partitions which separated the choir from the aisles. At the west end of the choir these stalls turned at right angles against the screen cutting the choir off from the rest of the church, leaving enough space in the middle for a processional entrance through the screen. In cathedrals of secular canons the vicars who substituted for the canons were usually accommodated in the lower row of stalls running in front of those of the canons. The four dignitaries had their stalls at the corners of the choir, while the bishop usually had his throne at the eastern end of the south rank of stalls. At Dunblane a number of the canons' stalls survive, dating from one of the three Chisholm episcopates between 1487 and 1569, though they are no longer in their original positions (**57**). They have the tip-up seats with ledges underneath known as misericords, which allowed the canons to lean comfortably against them while appearing to stand, and six of them still have the elaborate canopies which helped to reduce draughts and gave them architectural prominence.

The screen separating choir from nave was probably of timber in the majority of cathedrals, and integral with the backs of the stalls. We have some idea of how such screens could look from the parts of the screen surviving in the collegiate chapel of King's College in Aberdeen, while in the cathedral museum at Dunblane there are fragments of the arch through the screen from the nave into the choir. At Dunkeld there are slots in the chancel arch for the structural beams at the top of the screen. The screen at the west end of the choir was often known as the rood screen, because above it was the great rood or crucifix of the cathedral (see 56). This might be a painted scene of the crucifixion, or it could be in the form of three-dimensional carved figures of the crucified Christ flanked by the Virgin and St John. At Elgin the crucifixion was painted on boards, with a depiction of the last judgement behind it towards the choir, and it was destroyed only as late as 1640. We can understand how this would have looked from the remains of the crucifixion painting which came from above the screen at the collegiate church of Foulis Easter.

In monastic churches the main screen, which was frequently of stone, was known as a pulpitum, and the lowest courses of it still survive at St Andrews. Such stone screens were also built in at least one secular cathedral, because a very fine one survives complete at Glasgow (see 54). In many monastic churches there was a second screen in front of the pulpitum which could be of either stone or timber, and in such cases it was presumably the outer screen that had the rood above it. There was probably also an outer timber screen of this type at Glasgow, since a stair at the north-west corner of the nave has a doorway opening at what would have been the level of the loft on top of the screen. Lofts on screens and pulpita might have several functions. Often there would have been an altar dedicated to the holy rood there. Organs may also have been placed on the loft to accompany the singing, and these would have looked like the one depicted on the

altarpiece painted by Hugo Van Der Goes in the 1470s for Trinity College Chapel in Edinburgh, which is now displayed in the National Gallery of Scotland. From evidence elsewhere it seems there may sometimes even have been a third screen to enclose the altar or altars on the west side of the rood screen, though no examples of this are known of with certainty in Scotland.

Altars were the most frequently encountered fixtures in a medieval cathedral, although, since they were a particular target at the Reformation, the evidence for them is scanty. There is a rare survival at Glasgow, where the stone platforms for two altars added in front of the pulpitum by Archbishop Robert Blackadder (1483–1508) may still be seen (see 54). Useful pointers to the places in which some of the altars were sited can be aumbries (lockable wall cupboards) for the storage of some of the items used at the mass, and piscinae (recesses which usually have drained basins and often have decorated canopies) for washing the vessels used at mass. The altars themselves would have varied in scale but were usually of stone, with the flat slab known as the *mensa* carried on a solid masonry base, on small piers, or possibly cantilevered out from a wall or pier. The *mensa* usually had five crosses carved into its surface to signify the wounds of Christ, and there may have been a central recess within which relics could be sealed.

Behind an altar was usually a reredos or retable, frequently referred to as a tabernacle in the Middle Ages, which could be of stone or timber, and which usually had imagery relating to the dedication of the altar (see 56). Those of timber often had folding side wings which were able to be closed to protect the carvings or paintings when not in use. They were extremely expensive items, many being imported from the continent, and their donor might choose to be represented in supplication before the scenes that were represented. A portrait of Bishop William Elphinstone of Aberdeen with his hands clasped in prayer may be a fragment of such a retable. Pointers to the positions of altar retables can occasionally be found in the architecture. As they became more prominent as items of furnishing it might have been necessary to block the lower part of an existing window to accommodate them, though there was a growing tendency for the east walls of chapels to be built without windows so that they could be covered by retables. Traces of those once placed against the aisle end walls of Dunkeld nave can be seen in chases in the masonry, into which they could be secured. Also at the aisle ends of Dunkeld may be seen slots cut into the arcade piers for the screens enclosing those chapels.

The chapel occupying two bays at the east end of the south nave aisle at Dunkeld was particularly important because it was there that Bishop Robert Cardeny, who started the rebuilding of the nave in 1406, chose to be buried, and his canopied tomb was built into the south wall of the aisle (58). The chapel of Bishop John Winchester (1435–60) at the east of the south choir aisle of Elgin was of similar scale, and also contained his tomb (see 1), though most other chantries and side altars must have occupied far less space, and not all of them were enclosed by screens.

A favourite place for the tomb of a major benefactor, if it was still available, was on the north side of the presbytery. There it might have the additional function of providing a platform for the Easter Sepulchre or Tomb of Christ, which was where the consecrated host was symbolically entombed between Good Friday and Easter Sunday to signify Christ's own entombment. A gabled tomb in the north presbytery wall at Elgin which may have served this purpose was possibly provided for Bishop Archibald (1253–98), in whose time the cathedral was enlarged after the fire of 1270. At St Andrews, Bishop Henry Wardlaw (1403–40) placed his tomb in the north arcade, between the presbytery and Lady Chapel, towards the end of the long process of refurbishing the cathedral after the fire of 1378. But tombs in these areas could also serve other purposes. Another at Elgin on the north side of the

presbytery served additionally as a screen, with two sections of its three-gabled canopy covering the tomb, and a third covering the doorway from the aisle into the presbytery.

The Easter Sepulchre should not be confused with the Sacrament House, which was a more-or-less elaborate locker to the north or east of a principal altar. Bread that had been consecrated but not consumed at the mass, and was therefore regarded as being still the body of Christ, could be stored in Sacrament Houses for purposes of veneration, or for taking to the sick.

On the south side of the presbytery, sometimes corresponding to an Easter Sepulchre on the north, would usually have been sedilia, which were seats used by the celebrant and his assistants at certain points of the mass. Often these were of timber and have left no trace, though stone examples survive at Dunkeld, Elgin and Lismore. Those at Dunkeld and Lismore have three arched recesses, but the one at Elgin has four recesses surmounted by gablets. Other furnishings in the presbytery included lecterns (upright book desks) for the gospels and epistles. No movable lecterns survive in any of our cathedrals, though there used to be a brass eagle lectern at Holyrood Abbey, which was removed to a church in St Albans in England following the sack of the abbey by an English army in 1544. Clues to the positions of lecterns may occasionally survive, as at St Andrews, where there is a pair of slots in the presbytery steps into which one may have been fitted. (A different type of lectern survives at Elgin, where one of stone is built in with the central pier of the chapter house (see 52).)

Particular prominence was given to furnishings associated with shrines or reliquaries of saints, and there are partial remains of what may have been the arcaded base of one of the shrines of St Kentigern at Glasgow. As a focus of pilgrimage, this was probably sited in a feretory (shrine) chapel, behind the high altar, though other shrines may have been placed on altars dedicated to the saints whose relics they housed.

58 The tomb of Bishop Robert Cardeny (1398–1437) in his chantry chapel at Dunkeld Cathedral.

Another fixture was the baptismal font which, since it was for the benefit of layfolk, was placed in the nave, and usually near the west end in order to illustrate that baptism symbolized entry into the church. One of the few cathedrals still to have a medieval font is Fortrose, where an example with a simple panelled octagonal bowl has been re-set in the south chapel. We know from those surviving in other churches, however, that they could have carvings on the basin of appropriate scenes from the life of Christ, like that at the collegiate church of Foulis Easter, while others might have the arms of donors. As with some altars, the baptistery area may have been enclosed by carved and painted screens, and the font itself would have had a lockable lid – possibly of great elaboration – to prevent the theft of the holy water for sacrilegious purposes.

From such scant remains of furnishings we can still understand something of the rich setting of the services, and this information is supplemented by records of gifts by bishops and senior clergy to their cathedrals. At St Andrews there was a great refurnishing after the fire in 1378, when the choir stalls were paid for by Prior James Bisset (1393–1416), while the screen at the west end of the choir was provided by the vicar of the parish church, Canon William Bower. At Dunkeld, Bishop Lauder (1452–75) gave a magnificent altarpiece painted with twenty-four miracles of St Columba, as well as the choir stalls and the bishop's throne, while Bishop Brown (1483–1515) imported an altarpiece from the Netherlands, gave lecterns for the epistle and gospel and fitted out several altars. At Glasgow we have a list of the more portable items required to accompany the services in an 'Inventory of the ornaments, reliques, jewels, vestments and books' compiled in 1431–2; some of those listed would have been acquired after Bishop Glendinning taxed the cathedral clergy in 1401 to provide these items.

This list, incidentally, reminds us of the importance of richly embroidered vestments and liturgical hangings in the appearance of a major church. Vestments for use at mass and in processions, together with hangings for the altars, had to be provided in all of the colours that were required at the different seasons and feasts of the year, and many of these would have been gifts. One of the many processional vestments in the care of Glasgow's sacrist was described as 'a very precious cope of brown damask inwoven with gold, with golden images on the orphreys'; it had been given by Sir John Darnley of Darnley. Donors might even wish to have occasional use of vestments they had given, and an agreement of 1320 at Glasgow allowed a member of the Hamilton family to borrow vestments for a priest, deacon and subdeacon which had been donated to the altar of the Virgin in the cathedral, so that they could be used in a chapel at Hamilton.

In itemizing furnishings it must be remembered that painted decoration played a greater part than we would now expect. Most masonry would have been rendered or plastered and lime-washed, and internally the more important parts would have been decorated in colours, sometimes with scenes from the lives of the saints and from the Bible (see **colour plate 5**). Little of this survives, though in the tower at Dunkeld, which was used as an ecclesiastical court house, there are paintings of the judgement of Solomon, the woman taken in adultery and other judicial scenes (**59**); the vaulting above the room was also covered with figurative and decorative paintings. Fixtures and furnishings, whether of stone or timber, would have been similarly richly decorated, as at Elgin where Bishop Winchester's tomb has traces of paintings of angels in the protected area underneath the tomb canopy (see **1**), and reference has already been made to the painting of the crucifixion above the rood screen there.

Bishops' residences

Bishops and archbishops were among the great men of the kingdom, and maintained great

59 A painting of the judgement of Solomon from the consistory court room in the tower of Dunkeld Cathedral.

households. To reflect their high estate they were well housed, and had to be prepared to defend their possessions if necessary; consequently, they lived in a way that was very little different from the lay magnates. In addition to having a residence in the vicinity of their cathedral, they might have other residences on their estates elsewhere, which in some cases might be more aptly described as country houses. There are remains of episcopal castles at St Andrews, Dornoch, Dunblane and Kirkwall, while Glasgow's is known partly from early views and excavations. Among other residences there are remains of those of the bishops of Aberdeen at Fetternear, of the bishops of Argyll at Saddell, of the bishops of Dunkeld at Cramond, of the bishops of Moray at Spynie

and of the archbishops of St Andrews at Dairsie, Melgund and Monimail. However, we know that the wealthier bishops had more residences than have survived, and a list of the houses of Bishop William Lamberton of St Andrews (1297–1328) gives Inchmurdo, Monimail, Dairsie, Torry, Muckhart, Kettins, Monymusk, Liston, Lasswade and Stow, as well as St Andrews.

The earliest work on a bishop's residence to survive on a significant scale is at Kirkwall, where there are the lower walls of an elongated rectangular hall that could be as early as the twelfth century, and which was presumably under construction at the same time as the nearby cathedral (60). In the time of Bishop Robert Reid (1541–58) it was heightened and an impressive circular tower was added at one

60 The interior of the bishop's palace at Kirkwall.

of the corners towards the cathedral, by which time it was probably part of a quadrangular grouping of buildings.

The castle of the bishops (later the archbishops) of St Andrews was first built by Bishop Roger in about 1200, but was destroyed during the Wars of Independence before being reconstructed by Bishop Walter Trail in the late fourteenth century. Trail laid out his rebuilt castle as an irregular pentagon with towers at the angles and ranges running behind some or all of the curtain walls. There were eventually also outworks to the west of the main enclosure, and covering the entrance on the south side. As thus rebuilt, St Andrews Castle was both a handsome residence and a formidable place of strength; it was made even stronger in the early sixteenth century when two massive artillery blockhouses were built at the outer landward angles, probably by Archbishop James Beaton (1521–39). However, even the strongest defences were not proof against subterfuge or the most determined siege and, after his nephew, Cardinal David Beaton, had been murdered in the castle in 1546, the castle was taken following

bombardment by a French fleet. This led to further major rebuilding by Archbishop John Hamilton (1546–71), who created a French-inspired entrance range containing the bishop's own lodging, which was originally topped by a lavish array of gablets (see **colour plate 10**).

Few other episcopal castles had such an eventful history as that at St Andrews, though others were as strongly fortified. The main residence of the bishops of Moray at Spynie was another pentagonal enclosure surrounded by high walls and with towers at the angles (**61**). There the bishops eventually occupied one of the most massive tower-houses ever constructed in Scotland (see **colour plate 11**). It was built at a corner of the enclosure, apparently over an existing circular angle tower, by Bishops David Stewart and William Tulloch (successively 1462–82). Facing each other across the north and south sides of the courtyard were hall and chapel ranges, with the main gatehouse on the east. As at St Andrews, there were periodic efforts to up-date its defences, as seen in a number of very business-like gunholes inserted by Bishop Patrick Hepburn (1538–73).

A tower-house which was to the south-west of the cathedral may ultimately have been the main residential element of the castle of the archbishops of Glasgow, and a little about

61 A reconstruction sketch of how the castle of the bishops of Moray at Spynie may have appeared when complete (David Simon).

which is known from early views and recent excavations. Apart from the tower-house there was a high curtain wall surrounding the irregular site with at least one major angle tower, and there was also a large towered gatehouse. It is uncertain who built which parts and although Bishop John Cameron (1426–46) is usually said to have constructed the tower-house, he may have done no more than extend it. Archbishop James Beaton (1508–23) built much or all of the curtain wall together with the substantial tower at its north-west corner, and Archbishop Gavin Dunbar (1523–47) added the gatehouse, the heraldic panels from which are now preserved in the cathedral crypt. Yet another tower-house serving as the main element in an episcopal residence is at Saddell, in Argyll, which was built by Bishop David Hamilton, and which is unusual in having two rooms to each floor. It was built in 1508, after the estates of the nearby defunct Cistercian abbey had been transferred to the bishop, and perhaps in anticipation of a suggestion of 1512 that the abbey church should become the cathedral of the diocese in place of Lismore.

An effort to present some appearance of defensibility was also attempted at the episcopal residences in Dornoch and Dunblane. In both cases the buildings were ranged around more or less regular courtyards; at Dornoch the heavily restored south range is the main survivor, while at Dunblane there is only a vaulted undercroft above ground, although traces of other ranges have been found through excavation.

Cardinal David Beaton of St Andrews was a keen builder of impressive houses, and at Melgund in Angus there are substantial remains of a house which combines a tower-house and hall range as its main nucleus. However, this was not strictly an archiepiscopal residence, because it was built for Beaton's mistress, Marion Ogilvy, after he had acquired the estate in 1543, and was part of his attempt to make long-term provision for his family. After the cardinal's murder in 1546, Marion lived on at Melgund until her own death in 1575. Beaton is also traditionally associated with a building at Monimail in Fife, one of the country houses of the archbishops of St Andrews. The buildings were arranged around a quadrangular courtyard, which had its main range along the south side. The most complete remains are of a square tower which was built up against this range, and it is the lower storeys of this which are usually linked with Beaton, though its upper parts were added in 1578. Since such towers are inherently strong structures it is natural that they tend to be among the parts that survive when much else is gone. This is the case at a residence of the bishops of Dunkeld on an outlying part of their diocese at Cramond, west of Edinburgh, where a four-storeyed tower with a stair turret at one corner survives from a larger complex.

The residences of the other cathedral clergy

At the monastic cathedrals the canons regular were housed in the same way as at any other religious house, within three ranges of communal buildings around a cloister against the flank of the church nave. At Whithorn this cloister was on the north side of the cathedral, but little is known of its buildings other than some excavated walls of the east range. At St Andrews the cloister was more orthodox in having been on the south side of the nave, and parts of the stone-vaulted lower storeys of all three ranges have survived, though they underwent heavy restoration and rebuilding by the Marquess of Bute towards the end of the last century. As usual, the canons' dormitory was on the first floor of the east range, with a stair leading down into the transept of the church at the north end, and a latrine block over the great drain at the south end. Below the dormitory were various rooms, including the chapter house (the main meeting room of the canons), which had been rebuilt by Bishop Lamberton (1297–1328), and the warming room, where the canons could have the comfort of a fire during the colder parts of the year. The canons' refectory was above a vaulted undercroft, along

62 The manse of the chanter at Elgin Cathedral.

the south side of the cloister. The west range had various uses; as well as containing the senzie house, the meeting-hall for the synod of the diocese, the sub-prior may have had his lodging here. Within the wider precinct were many other buildings, including guest houses, barns and mills, and the whole was enclosed by a wall which survives for much of its length, and which still has thirteen towers and four gateways.

At the secular cathedrals most of the canons would have had individual manses within the cathedral close, known as the chanonry. Few manses survive, though we know the approximate layouts of several of the chanonries. Responsibility for building the manses evidently rested with the individual prebendaries and, in view of the levels of absenteeism, it is not surprising that maintenance was a recurring problem. In 1489 at Elgin orders were given to repair the manses, with fines threatened if this were not done. At Dunkeld many of the manses were arranged along the two sides of what is now High Street, and this must have given the chanonry a rather urban appearance. But in other cases the manses were free-standing buildings, looking like urban tower-houses, set back behind high garden walls. The best surviving example is the so-called bishop's house at Elgin, which was probably the manse of the chanter (precentor) (**62**). It reached its final state by 1557, but incorporates work of a number of periods. The main element was a rectangular block with a hall at first-floor level, which was connected to a smaller chamber block by stair tower. Another house, which seems to have been a prebendal manse, is the building known as Provand's Lordship in Glasgow, and other manses survived there into the nineteenth century (**63**).

From regulations at Elgin and Aberdeen, it seems an incoming canon would expect to have basic household furnishing and equipment passed on to him with his manse, including a trestle table, a bed with a tester and items necessary for cooking, eating and sleeping. The clearest pointer to the comfortable life-style of a better-endowed prebendary is an inventory of 1542 of the possessions of the recently deceased Canon Adam Colquhoun of Glasgow, who held the prebend of Stobo, and whose manse survived in a much-modified state until 1852.

The rooms and outbuildings listed for Canon Adam's manse were the oratory, the hall, his

63 One of the manses of the canons of Glasgow Cathedral as it had survived into the later nineteenth century (Fairbairn, *Relics of ancient architecture ... in Glasgow*, 1885).

chamber, the kitchen and brewhouse, a barn and a stable. The contents of his oratory included precious altar silver and books valued at £100, though the only vestments and hangings were of black, suggesting that most of the masses he offered were for the dead. In the hall was a dining table and its linen cloths; around the table were finely carved seats, benches and stools. There was also a canopied cupboard for linen and a larger carved cupboard on which was displayed a great amount of silver; a number of items, including a dozen cushions, are specified as being of Flemish workmanship. The centrepiece of the bedchamber was a carved and gilded bed with costly sheets, covers and damask hangings, while there were chests and presses for storage, and the room was lit by a hanging chandelier. In addition, various items of expensive clothing and valuables were stored here, and – rather more intriguingly – there was a parrot valued at £10. Further aspects of the canon's life are illuminated by the list of his personal armour and his sporting equipment for archery, hare-coursing and hunting. He also owned a chiming clock. Apart from the oratory and his clerical clothing, there is little here to mark Canon Adam as different from any other wealthy burgess. This impression is reinforced when we learn from other sources that he lived with a

mistress and had at least two illegitimate sons (it seems the holders of this prebend were not distinguished for piety, because in 1501–2 his predecessor was formally censured for his irreverent behaviour: wandering in and out of the choir during services).

Colquhoun must have been one of the better-endowed canons, though his quality of life was probably not exceptional, and it must have offered a contrast to the life of the vicars choral who carried much of the daily burden of the cathedral services. Initially each vicar was probably housed by the canon he served, who was also responsible for paying him and for providing his choir vestments. But eventually a separate enclave for the vicars was usually built within the chanonries, with individual residences together with rooms used in common. At Glasgow the vicars' close was to the north of the cathedral, where there was a communal hall and a kitchen reached across a bridge from the cathedral sacristy. In general, cathedral chapters adopted a rather lofty attitude towards the vicars, as at Aberdeen, where it was ordered that the gates to their close were to be locked at 8.00 p.m. in the winter and 9.00 p.m. in the summer. In the later Middle Ages, however, there seems to have been some difficulty in recruiting vicars until their pay was increased and they were granted greater security of tenure.

5
The cathedrals since the Reformation

The early stages of the Reformation

The Reformation was less a single event than a development unfolding over many decades, though the great watershed was the parliament of August 1560, which repudiated the pope as head of the Church and abolished the mass as its central act of worship. For the more committed reformers, bishops were seen as perpetuating the hierarchies of the old Church, and the First Book of Discipline of June 1560 envisaged a more logically planned geographical distribution of dioceses headed by a new breed of leaders to be known as superintendents. In fact there were major problems in achieving this plan, for although the bishops of Galloway, Caithness and Orkney conformed to the new religion others did not, and there was no mechanism for getting rid of the latter. Additionally, successive monarchs and regents favoured episcopacy as an aid to centralized control of the Church. But beyond all of that, the chronic shortage of funds suffered by the reformed Church meant it was difficult to finance radically new measures.

Bishops thus continued to exist in an uneasy relationship with superintendents, though in the new Church they did not enjoy the authority and standing of their pre-Reformation counterparts. Indeed, they were to be disparagingly dismissed by their detractors as 'tulchans', a reference to the dummy calves used by farmers to encourage cows to give milk, since part of the income the bishops might have expected was often diverted

to other uses – a practice that was by no means new. Under these circumstances, and without an elaborate liturgy to perform, there was little need for them to have large and richly furnished cathedral churches. In some cases, when a cathedral city had a separate parish church, as at St Andrews and Elgin, the cathedral was simply rejected in favour of the smaller church (**64**), though at Old Aberdeen a parish church was abandoned in favour of the cathedral. In most other cases the cathedrals were retained in use, at least for the time being, though the emphasis on preaching in the new forms of worship called for spaces that were essentially auditoria, and this often meant retention of only part of the building, as at Dunkeld (see **35**). The physical impact of the Reformation on the cathedrals will be further considered below.

Episcopacy and Presbyterianism

In all of this it is doubtful how far churches used by bishops could still be called cathedrals in any real sense, and for a while this was to become even more doubtful as the more radical reformers began to argue that there was no place at all for bishops in the new Church. A leading advocate of abolition was Andrew Melville, who had studied in France and Geneva, and who is perhaps unfairly best remembered for pointing out to James VI with something less than consummate tact that he was no more than 'God's sillie vassal'. Under his guidance the General Assembly had by 1581

64 Elgin Cathedral in the later seventeenth century, after it had been abandoned for worship (Slezer, *Theatrum Scotiae*, 1693).

resolved to do away with bishops in favour of a Presbyterian four-fold system of ecclesiastical courts. But this was too much for the king, and in 1584 the 'Black Acts' re-established his authority over the Church and strengthened the position of bishops. Although the Acts were repealed in 1592, the process of restoring episcopacy was complete by 1610.

Through most of these changes the essentially Protestant forms of worship now practised remained unchanged and, however the Church was ruled, bishops co-existed with presbyteries in a way that might now seem incompatible. But a period of further change was ahead. James VI, who in 1603 had become king of England as well as of Scotland, admired the Church in his new kingdom, and hoped to bring his Church in Scotland more into line with the Church south of the Border. At the 1618 Assembly in Perth he tried to introduce a more Anglican approach to worship through what were known as the Five Articles. However, James – who knew the

temper of his Scottish subjects well enough – was soon made to realize that he had gone too far in this and did not press the matter excessively.

Unfortunately Charles I, who succeeded his father in 1625, was less sensitive in his dealings with Scotland. At the time of his 'homecoming' for his Scottish coronation in 1633, he offended many through the ceremonial of the service, and it soon also became apparent that he had firm plans for the Scottish Church which included a formal liturgy and a strong system of episcopacy based on the English model. To complement this he wished to restore the cathedrals and the estates of the bishops. At Iona, for example, the eastern parts of the abbey church were partly restored for use as the cathedral of the diocese of the Isles (**65** and **colour plate 12**). At St Andrews what remained of the archiepiscopal estates was purchased from the Duke of Lennox and granted to the archbishops, though they continued to use the parish church as their cathedral. Among the king's other acts was the establishment of a new diocese of Edinburgh, based on the burgh church of St Giles (**66**). Charles's efforts galvanized opposition, both

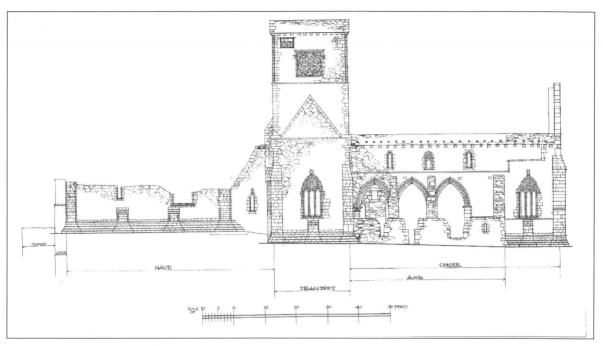

65 Iona Abbey before modern restoration (National Art Survey of Scotland, 1921–33).

66 Edinburgh St Giles before nineteenth-century restoration (Laing, *Registrum ... Sancti Egidii de Edinburgh*, 1859).

from those who had no wish for religious change as well as from those who feared they might lose out in the effort to re-endow the Church. In 1638 the National Covenant was signed in opposition to innovations in worship, and later in the same year the General Assembly at Glasgow abolished bishops and service books and reintroduced presbyterianism. But the king's plans for the Church were halted by the outbreak of the Civil War in England, which eventually led to his execution.

After the monarchy was restored throughout Britain in 1660, bishops were reintroduced by the Act Rescissory of 1661; four new Scottish bishops were consecrated at Westminster, and consecrated their brother bishops on their return. Unfortunately, however, there was a new bitterness in Church affairs and, though there were few changes to the forms of worship, there was much resistance to the bishops themselves. In the reign of James VII, there was a yet further twist to the story, since James was openly Catholic and anxious to grant freedom to his co-religionists. Events in England led to James's flight at the end of 1688, and he was replaced on the throne by his daughter, Mary, and her husband, William of Orange. William and Mary were presumably as favourable to bishops in Scotland as they were in England, but the hearts of some of the bishops stayed with James VII. In the face of lukewarm assurances of loyalty from the bishops, in 1689 William and Mary finally abolished episcopacy from the national Church, and bishops no longer had any place in their cathedral churches.

Yet, despite the difficulties and dangers, considerable numbers chose to remain faithful to the idea of a reformed Church governed by bishops, and these were the first members of what was to become the Episcopal Church, some of whom were to suffer great hardship for their allegiance. This was even more the case after the death of Queen Anne and the succession of the Hanoverian dynasty in 1714, because many in the Episcopal Church continued to support the direct male heirs of the deposed James VII, despite the fact that those heirs were Catholic. After the rebellions of 1715 and 1719 only clergy prepared to 'qualify' by taking an oath of abjuration were allowed to practise freely, and they passed under the authority of the English Church rather than the Scottish bishops. Difficulties were also developing amongst the bishops themselves. In 1704 it had been decided that new bishops should not be appointed to specific dioceses, and in 1720 they agreed to form themselves into a college with a president who took the title of Primus. Inevitably, a division grew up between those who considered themselves as diocesan bishops and those who saw themselves as part of the college. Even greater problems followed the Rising of 1745 and, with the further crippling penalties then imposed, the Episcopal Church seemed to be in terminal decline.

The physical impact of the Reformation and its aftermath on the cathedrals

As a result of events since 1560, of the thirteen medieval cathedrals only five are now structurally virtually entire, while three others have one of their parts still in use. The five that are structurally complete are Brechin, Dornoch, Dunblane, Glasgow and Kirkwall, though it should be said that the first three of those are only so complete because substantial parts were rebuilt in the nineteenth or early twentieth centuries; the three that are partly in use are Aberdeen, Dunkeld and Lismore. The remaining five, which are no longer in any use for worship and are in varying states of ruination, are Elgin, Fortrose, St Andrews, Snizort and Whithorn. In order to understand something of how the cathedrals attained their present state, three of them will be considered a little more closely: Glasgow, Aberdeen and Elgin.

The post-Reformation histories of the cathedrals varied considerably, though all of them were largely 'cleansed' of the furnishings of medieval worship in the build-up to or soon after the Reformation. St Andrews, for example, was cleansed following a sermon preached by

John Knox in the parish church on 11 June 1559. Nevertheless, in more conservative parts of the country some furnishings survived for a remarkably long time, even if they were no longer the foci of worship, as at Aberdeen, where the altar of St Catherine in the south transept survived to about the mid-seventeenth century. It should be stressed, however, that the leaders of the reformers probably had no wish to cause structural damage to the churches, since they saw that it was very likely they would themselves wish to use the buildings; their wish was to remove what they saw as offensive trappings of a form of worship that they believed it their duty to extirpate. But, as with all such movements, it was no easy task to curb the activities of all the more zealous followers and, beyond that, there were inevitably some who were willing to take advantage of a volatile situation to purloin valuable building materials.

At Glasgow, Archbishop James Beaton had attempted to meet the oncoming storm to some extent by protecting the archdiocese's property through an arrangement with the Earl of Arran, but unfortunately Arran almost immediately elected to associate himself with the reformers' cause and soon occupied the archbishop's castle. Beaton fled to Paris in July 1560 though, as one indicator of how unpredictable the course of events might be, as late as 1598 he was to be nominally restored to office in reward for his services to James VI. For many years there were to be great difficulties in obtaining the services of reformed ministers in Glasgow and Mary Queen of Scots, who herself remained staunchly Catholic, in 1567 provided endowments to assist the burgh in appointing a reformed minister to the parish. His relationship with the rest of the cathedral establishment must initially have been rather difficult, however, since as late as 1572 only six of the prebendaries of the chapter were Protestant. A second minister was appointed to the parish in 1587, a third in 1592 and a fourth in 1595.

Of these four ministers, all but the third used the cathedral for their services. Major changes thus had to be made to permit the building to be used simultaneously by the three congregations, and the records of the town council in 1574 show that by then much structural work was also needed, due to the decay brought about by the earlier removal of roof coverings. The first congregation eventually occupied what had been the canons' choir, which came to be known as the inner high kirk, and a wall to enclose this part of the building had been constructed by no later than 1635. The second congregation came to occupy the five western bays of the nave, which was known as the outer high kirk, and a second wall to separate off this part was constructed in 1647. The unenclosed eastern bays of the nave and the transepts came to be known rather misleadingly as 'the choir', though this area served as little more than a vestibule for the other parts of the building, and an entrance doorway was cut into it through the south nave aisle wall for this purpose. The third congregation was the barony kirk, which was housed in the crypt below the choir.

With the strong emphasis placed on preaching by the reformed Church, congregations needed spaces which would allow as many as possible to be within hearing distance of the pulpit and, in addition to subdividing older churches to provide more manageable spaces, a further way of achieving this was to construct timber galleries, thus creating upper levels of seating. At Glasgow they were being built within the aisles of the nave by 1647, and in the choir by 1649. It is likely that the placing of these galleries initially showed relatively little sense of order, however, and it was only in 1805 that those in the choir were rebuilt to a more architecturally regular pattern.

However unsuitable the post-Reformation internal subdivision and addition of galleries in a cathedral might seem to modern visitors, such adaptation at Glasgow did at least ensure that it was the only mainland cathedral to survive in a structurally complete state into the nineteenth century, by when changed attitudes to the past

101

meant it was far more likely that a great medieval building would be preserved on account of its own merits. At Glasgow the inappropriateness of the subdivisions began to be perceived as early as the turn of the eighteenth century, and the barony kirk congregation was removed from the crypt in 1798, followed by the removal of the outer high kirk congregation from the nave in 1835. The last of the galleries were eventually removed in 1852.

Subdivision was also the approach adopted at Aberdeen to meet the needs of the parishioners there but, although the congregations of both the cathedral parish and that of St Mary de Nives had to be housed, there was ultimately no need to retain the entire building. In any case, it is by no means certain that there was an entire building to be retained, since it is not clear if the rebuilding of the choir initiated by Bishop Elphinstone before his death in 1514 had ever been completed. As at Glasgow, Bishop Gordon of Aberdeen made an attempt on the eve of the Reformation to protect some of the wealth of his cathedral, in this case by entrusting many of its treasures both to the canons and to the Earl of Huntly, the latter remaining more firmly Catholic than the Earl of Arran at Glasgow, and in the short term this was probably a successful move. The protection of the earl was also an advantage when a Protestant force reached the cathedral in January 1560, because some of the worst excesses of 'cleansing' were probably prevented through his intervention, and some furnishings even survived into the seventeenth century.

Aberdeen's greatest problems were probably caused by orders given by the Privy Council in 1568, at a time of national economic crisis, that the lead was to be stripped from the roofs and, though there is a grim irony in the fact that the ship carrying the lead (together with that from Elgin) sank on leaving harbour, this left the cathedral in an exposed condition. The nave was eventually covered by slates on the orders of the kirk session in 1607, though funds may not have stretched to slating other parts, and it may have been one result of the removal of the

lead in 1568 that the spire over the central tower collapsed. It was then replaced by a saddle-back roof. In 1638 the northernmost of the two transepts, which was presumably not needed for worship, was sold to the Marquess of Huntly as a family burial place, and this may have provided funds for further works of repair, because in 1642–4 the nave was again reslated, and work then followed on the transepts and central tower. In 1687, however, it became apparent that the central tower was in a dangerous state and, despite some ill-conducted remedial works, it fell in the following year, destroying much of the transepts and damaging parts of the nave. After that a wall was built across the east end of the nave and, despite occasional suggestions that the abandoned parts of the cathedral should be rebuilt – as was to be done at Brechin, Dornoch and Dunblane – this was never put into effect.

At Aberdeen one parish church had been abandoned in favour of the cathedral; at Elgin, however, it was the cathedral that was abandoned in favour of the local parish church of St Giles. The cathedral was probably 'cleansed' in 1561, if not before, and, as at Aberdeen, its roofs were stripped of their lead in 1568. In a change of heart the Privy Council ordered that it should be reroofed in 1569 and Bishop Patrick Hepburn offered to contribute to the costs, though nothing seems to have been done at the time and, apart from occasional acts of both Protestant and Catholic worship, the building was put to little use. With virtually no maintenance being carried out, it is hardly surprising that the choir roof blew down in the winter storms of December 1637. Nevertheless, as Slezer's engraving shows, much of the shell of the building continued to stand into the late seventeenth century (see **64**). To an even greater extent than at Aberdeen, where there was a congregation to care for its place of worship, the greatest single disaster at Elgin was the collapse of the central tower. This took place on Easter Sunday in 1711, destroying much of the nave and parts of the choir and transepts.

For nearly a century the building that must be regarded as one of the most beautiful ever raised in Scotland continued to decay, and it was only with the appointment in 1807 of John Shanks as keeper that this process was halted, and the cathedral began to be preserved as a widely admired ruin.

The revival of the Episcopalian and Roman Catholic Churches

The death in 1788 of the last major Jacobite claimant to the throne, Prince Charles Edward Stuart (Bonnie Prince Charlie), was a turning-point for the Episcopal Church. In that same year a synod in Aberdeen agreed to pray for George III, and in 1789 a party of bishops went to London to plead for the repeal of the punitive legislation. As a first stage, in 1792 the penal laws were repealed for those clergy who would subscribe to the Oath of Allegiance, and eventually all restrictions on Episcopalian clergy were lifted in 1864.

The process was also under way by which members of the Roman Catholic Church were to regain freedom to worship openly. The hierarchy of Catholic bishops had technically ended with the death in Paris of Archbishop James Beaton of Glasgow in 1603. After that, Scotland's Catholics had no bishop until Thomas Nicholson was appointed Vicar Apostolic in 1695, with the title of Bishop of Peristachium. He was based at Preshome in Banffshire, an area where Catholicism still had a strong hold. In 1727 two separate vicariates apostolic were set up, serving the Highlands and the Lowlands, and the holders of these offices similarly held the rank of bishop. Catholic worship was still then a criminal offence, but in 1793 the passing of the Catholic Relief Act permitted greater freedom. In 1827 three vicariates were set up, for the east, the west and the north, based on Edinburgh, Glasgow and Preshome. Soon after that, the situation improved yet further with the passing of the Catholic Emancipation Act of 1829. Nevertheless, Scottish Catholics were still

concerned not to antagonize their compatriots, and the time was not yet deemed ripe to restore diocesan bishops. It was probably only a period of instability within the Church following the influx of large numbers of Irish in the 1840s which led to the decision to restore a full diocesan hierarchy. In 1867 it was suggested that two archdioceses and six dioceses should be established, and this was eventually implemented in 1878. In 1948 two further dioceses were created to serve the areas around Glasgow, where the number of Catholics was particularly great.

In 1792 and 1878, therefore, Scotland came to have two legally recognized bodies of diocesan bishops who, despite having no part in the established Church of Scotland, were to play a very active role in Church life. But, although the revitalized Episcopal and Roman Catholic Churches were great builders, in each case it would be a little time before their bishops felt able to provide themselves with buildings formally designated as cathedrals. Before looking at those new cathedrals, however, it would be as well to consider what was happening at this period to the cathedrals that had been constructed in the Middle Ages.

The renewal of interest in the medieval cathedrals

One consequence of the abolition of bishops within the national Church in 1689 had been that the buildings and endowments associated with episcopacy had passed to the crown. So far as the buildings were concerned this meant very little at first, and most continued to be used at least partly for worship. However, as interest in medieval architecture grew, it was occasionally possible to persuade the crown to contribute towards the repair of cathedral buildings, and particularly those that were no longer in use. In 1762, for example, money was given towards work on the tower of Dunkeld, while in 1789 the state paid for the stabilization of St Rule's church at St Andrews through the Barons of the Exchequer (see **3**). Greater impetus was given to this process in 1824 when Robert Reid, who already bore the honorary title of King's Architect in Scotland, headed a shortlived separate Scottish Office of Works. He reported on the needs of a number of medieval buildings – both ruined and in use – that were assumed to be crown property.

The spur to action was often local pressure, though Reid and his successors were usually keen to put the case for government action. At Elgin a local man, John Shanks, had been appointed keeper of the site in 1807, and devoted much of the rest of his life to clearing out the ruins single-handedly (**67**); although we can now see that this caused great loss of evidence, this should not detract from Shanks's achievement. It was only later that the state became involved at Elgin, with Reid preparing reports on necessary works of stabilization in 1824 and 1834. At St Andrews Cathedral, where clearance of the ruins had been started in 1824, Reid argued in 1837 that the state should

assume full responsibility for the site and the keepers appointed to look after it, and this was eventually accepted. Ultimately the state accepted responsibility for the abandoned cathedrals of Elgin, Fortrose, St Andrews and Whithorn (**68** and **colour plate 9**), and for the unused parts of Aberdeen, Brechin and Dunkeld Cathedrals. But state interest was not limited to abandoned or disused cathedral structures, and responsibility was also assumed eventually for the entire buildings at Glasgow and Dunblane Cathedrals, both of which remain in use for worship (see **19**, **28**).

So far as the cathedrals in continuing use were concerned, the major turning-point in the growth of state involvement was a far-reaching programme of work at Glasgow, where there had been pleas for restoration since 1833, and in which Robert Reid became involved in 1836. It came to be accepted that the crown had financial responsibility for structurally necessary works, though proposals to replace the asymmetrical western towers with structures regarded as more appropriate were deemed to be a local responsibility. By 1857 it was agreed the crown should become responsible for the

67 Elgin Cathedral in the course of clearance operations, with John Shanks, the keeper, explaining the site to visitors (Forsyth, *A series of views ... of Elgin Cathedral*, 1826).

The nave of Whithorn Cathedral from the south-east. The transepts used to be where there is now the gable wall on the right.

whole of Glasgow Cathedral. However, the extent of and justification for the state's role in such buildings was not always understood. In the later 1840s an expensive campaign of restoration was carried out on Kirkwall Cathedral, though it was only when the work was nearing completion that the burgh established that the building was its own rather than the state's by virtue of a grant of James III (**69**).

As the nineteenth century progressed, renewed pride in the nation's architectural past led to repairs and restoration being carried out at all of the cathedrals in use, even if some of the earlier operations seem rather drastic to modern eyes. The demolition of Glasgow's west towers in 1846 and 1848, William Burn's recasing of Edinburgh in 1829–33 and Alexander Coupar's restoration of Dornoch in 1835–7 all resulted in significant destruction of

information, despite the underlying good intentions. The same is true of Archibald Elliot's restoration of Dunkeld in 1814–15, and Gillespie Graham's remodelling of the choir of Dunblane in 1816–19 (**70**). But we should remember that the cathedrals were not then regarded as irreplaceable documents of the past as we now see them, so much as beautiful buildings that had been damaged and could be made even more beautiful at a time when artistic taste was believed to have become so much more enlightened. In the course of the century, however, restoring architects increasingly adopted a more careful approach towards the preservation of historic fabric. Despite the qualms of the Society for the

69 Kirkwall Cathedral in the course of restoration (Billings, *The baronial and ecclesiastical antiquities of Scotland*, 1845–52).

70 Dunblane Cathedral after its restoration by James Gillespie Graham but before the re-roofing of the nave (compare with **33**).

71 Perth Episcopal Cathedral.

Protection of Ancient Buildings, Sir Robert Rowand Anderson's restoration of Dunblane in 1889–93, which also embraced the re-roofing of the nave, was probably as sensitive an operation as anything of its kind (see 28). John Honeyman's restoration of Brechin in 1900–2 was less authoritatively based, but in that case there was limited surviving evidence, and the

architect did at least produce architecture that was historically plausible (see 12).

The new cathedrals of the nineteenth and twentieth centuries

Lifting penalties against the Episcopal and Roman Catholic churches released vast stores of energy and fostered a missionary enthusiasm which resulted in a great deal of new building. Some of the churches founded in the main centres of population were conceived on such a scale that it might be suspected there were hopes from the start of eventually designating them as cathedrals, though relatively few were actually built as such. Both denominations adopted a pattern of dioceses which took their names from those of medieval or Caroline creation, though the cathedrals were sometimes placed in more appropriate cities. For the Episcopal Church there were to be cathedrals in Perth (71) (dioceses of St Andrews, Dunkeld and Dunblane), Aberdeen, Dundee (diocese of Brechin), Edinburgh, Glasgow, Inverness (72) (dioceses of Moray, Ross and Caithness) and

72 Inverness Episcopal Cathedral (Crown Copyright: Royal Commission on the Ancient and Historical Monuments of Scotland).

73 Glasgow Roman Catholic Cathedral (Crown Copyright: Royal Commission on the Ancient and Historical Monuments of Scotland).

This resulted in some fine buildings, though it was in some ways unfortunate since it fostered a growing – but historically inaccurate – perception that the Episcopal Church was the 'English Church in Scotland'. It was particularly significant that in 1849 William Butterfield was called up to design the first cathedral to be built as such since the Reformation, at Perth (see **71**). In the same year he also designed the church and theological college at Millport on the Isle of Cumbrae, which was to be the cathedral of Argyll and the Isles between 1876 and 1920. A leading spirit behind both of these projects was the future sixth Earl of Glasgow, who developed a taste for High Anglican churchmanship in his time at Christ Church, Oxford. The Perth Cathedral project was highly controversial because it was the Episcopal Church's first purpose-built cathedral, and some felt the time

74 Aberdeen Roman Catholic Cathedral (Crown Copyright: Royal Commission on the Ancient and Historical Monuments of Scotland).

Oban (dioceses of Argyll and the Isles). There is also a church at Cumbrae which served the dioceses of Argyll and the Isles for a while before Oban took over this role. For the Catholic Church there were eventually cathedrals of two archdioceses at Edinburgh (for St Andrews and Edinburgh) and Glasgow (**73**), with the other cathedrals at Aberdeen (**74**), Ayr (diocese of Galloway, originally centred on Dumfries), Dundee (diocese of Dunkeld), Motherwell, Oban (dioceses of Argyll and the Isles) and Paisley. The two additions to the medieval and seventeenth-century dioceses were those based at Motherwell and Paisley, which were created as suffragans of Glasgow in 1948.

The oldest of the buildings which came to serve as a cathedral for the Episcopal Church was at Aberdeen, which was designed by the important local architect Archibald Simpson in 1816, though it was only elevated to cathedral status in 1914; later, however, there was a tendency for many of the major Episcopal churches to be designed by English architects.

was not yet appropriate for it to be built; it was also feared it would divert funds from another major project, a theological college and school founded in 1847 at Glenalmond in Perthshire.

Another English architect favoured by the Episcopal Church was Sir George Gilbert Scott. He designed the most ambitious of the new cathedrals, St Mary's in Edinburgh, which was built between 1874 and 1917. Scott also designed the churches that became the cathedrals in Dundee and Glasgow (and did some work on the medieval cathedral of Dunblane). But not all the Episcopalian cathedral projects went to English architects. Alexander Ross, one of the defeated entrants in the competition for building Edinburgh Cathedral, had earlier received the commission for building Inverness Cathedral in 1866, the twin towers of which figure so prominently in the city's skyline (see **72**).

As already said, nearly all of the Catholic cathedrals were originally built as chapels or parish churches, including those of the archdioceses of Edinburgh and Glasgow, which were only formally designated as cathedrals in 1878 and 1889 respectively (see **73**). Both were large-scale churches originally designed by James Gillespie Graham, in 1813 and 1814, and it is certainly easier to appreciate his merits as an architect in those works than in his proposals for improving the medieval cathedral of Glasgow, or in his restoration of Dunblane. The only Catholic cathedral to be built as such was at Oban, which was started in 1932, though in

some other cases there was some rebuilding or enlargement when cathedral status was achieved or in sight. At Aberdeen, for example, the spire was built shortly before it became a cathedral in 1878 (see **74**), though in this connection it should be remembered that Catholic churches were supposed not to have spires or bells until this absurd restriction was removed in 1926.

More recently Scotland has acquired a Greek Orthodox cathedral in Glasgow, where a church built for a United Presbyterian congregation has been converted for this purpose.

As a consequence of all of this building activity, Scotland now has sixteen functioning cathedrals (seventeen if Cumbrae is included). But in addition, although none of the medieval or Caroline cathedrals is strictly a cathedral in the sense of being a bishop's church, a tempering of attitudes in the Scottish Church means that the nine (including Edinburgh, but ten if Iona is also included) which are still wholly or partly in use are again often described as cathedrals. Thus, from having had no cathedrals at all between 1689 and 1849, Scotland now has twenty-seven churches in use bearing the title, and there is the fascinating situation that Glasgow has four cathedrals, Aberdeen and Edinburgh three cathedrals, and Dundee has two. Brief details of all of these buildings, and of a number of the sites that have been associated with bishops at some stage of their history, will be found in the gazetteer which follows this chapter.

Gazetteer

Cathedrals of medieval foundation are listed in bold capitals, while those of post-Reformation and modern foundation are given in lighter capitals. Names of buildings or sites which were or may have been connected in some way with a medieval cathedral or bishop's church are given in brackets, though the choice of these is selective since the gazetteer is not intended to provide a complete list of medieval episcopal sites (**75**).

On the plans, surviving medieval work is shown in solid black, modern work by open lines and missing work by broken lines.

(ABERCORN, ST WILFRED, West Lothian) A mid-seventh-century monastic church here was briefly used as his cathedral by the Anglian Bishop Trumwine in the 680s, though he was forced to abandon it after the defeat of the Anglians by the Picts at the battle of Nechtansmere in 685. The main surviving evidence for the continued existence of an early ecclesiastical foundation is an important collection of carved fragments of the eighth century or later. The present church, which remains in use, is a parochial structure of twelfth-century date, though much of its appearance dates from major reconstructions in 1579 and 1893, with various other additions.

ABERDEEN, CATHEDRAL OF ST MACHAR (76 and see **43, 44, 55**) The cathedral is thought to have been moved from Mortlach to Aberdeen in about 1131 by Bishop Nechtan, though there is nothing in the present building before the later fourteenth century. In 1157 Bishop Edward was given permission to introduce either monks or canons to serve his cathedral, but little seems to have been done then, and it is likely the local clergy performed this function for a while. A chapter of secular canons begins to appear from the mid-thirteenth century, and eventually there were thirty canons supported by twenty-four vicars. The outline of the cathedral's building history was chronicled by Hector Boece, principal of the nearby King's College, in his account of the lives of the bishops of 1522. The most complete surviving part is the eight-bay aisled nave, which has a pair of spired towers over its western bays and a two-storeyed porch on its south flank. The lower walls of the transepts also survive, but the choir and central tower are gone. The nave was started by the second Bishop Alexander Kinninmund (1355–80); it was completed and the central tower started by Bishop Henry Lichton (1422–40), who also started to rebuild the north transept. Bishop Ingram Lindsay (1441–58) paved and roofed the nave. Much furnishing was provided by Bishop Thomas Spens (1457–80), and Bishop William Elphinstone (1483–1514) completed the central tower and transepts and started to rebuild the choir on a larger scale. Bishop Gavin Dunbar (1518–32) added the spires to the western towers and placed the heraldic ceiling over the nave. After the Reformation the nave was maintained for worship, being reslated in 1607 and again reroofed in the 1640s. The central tower fell in 1688, destroying the transepts. The nave remains in use and the shell of the transepts is in the care of Historic Scotland.

ABERDEEN, EPISCOPAL CATHEDRAL OF ST ANDREW The church which came to serve as the Episcopal cathedral in 1914 was started for Bishop John Skinner in 1816. (It was Skinner who, as Primus, took the lead in showing the loyalty of his church to the Hanoverian dynasty after the death of the Young Pretender in 1788, which eventually led to the lifting of the penal laws.) His church is an aisled building in the English perpendicular style designed by Archibald Simpson. A chancel was added by George Edmund Street in 1880, and a porch and screen by Sir Robert Lorimer in 1911. Further major reordering and refurnishing was carried out by Sir Ninian Comper between 1935 and 1943.

ABERDEEN, ROMAN CATHOLIC CATHEDRAL OF ST MARY (see **74**) The chapel, which became the Catholic cathedral in 1878, was built by Alexander Ellis in 1860 in a fourteenth-century style. It has an

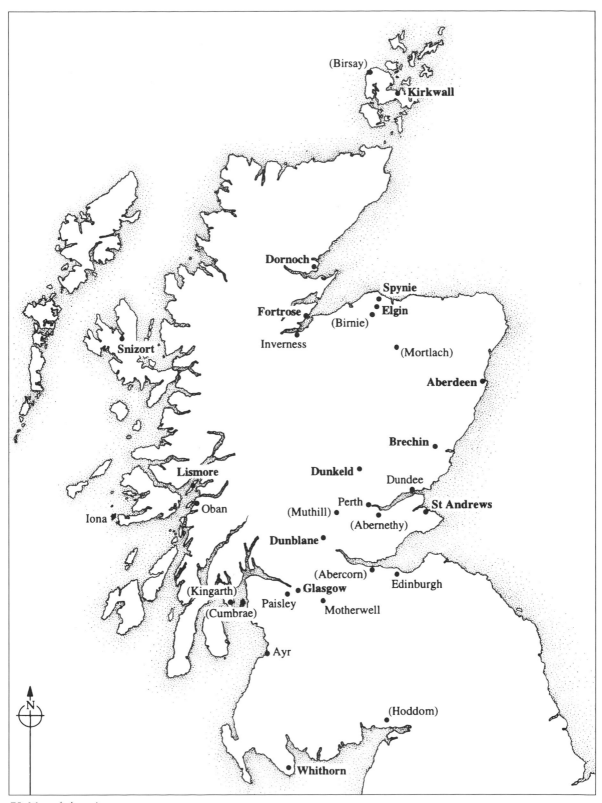

75 Map of places in gazetteer

aisled nave and short chancel. The finest feature is the steeple, rising to more than 60 metres (around 200ft), which was completed by R.G. Wilson shortly before the church was elevated to cathedral status.

(ABERNETHY, ST BRIGID, Perthshire) Abernethy was a capital of Pictland, and was possibly the seat of a short-lived bishopric founded by King Nechtan in the eighth century. The continuing existence of some form of community is indicated by early carved stones, and also by the existence of a round tower of Irish type, which probably dates mainly from the years around 1100, but which has earlier work at its base. The tower is in the care of Historic Scotland.

AYR, ROMAN CATHOLIC CATHEDRAL OF THE GOOD SHEPHERD The cathedral which serves the diocese of Galloway was built to the designs of Fred Torry in 1955. The diocese was originally centred on Dumfries, but was relocated to Ayr after the cathedral there was burned in 1962. It was extensively refurnished in 1985.

(BIRNIE, ST BRENDAN, Moray) (see 7) A diocese in Moray was possibly established in the eleventh century by the mormaers (local rulers) of the province, though the area increasingly came under royal control from the 1130s. The seat of the earlier bishops was variously at Birnie, Kinneddar and Spynie, until fixed at Spynie in 1207–8 and then at Elgin in 1224. The church at Birnie, which remains in use, dates from around the second quarter of the twelfth century, and may have been the building that was sometimes used by the bishops. It is a two-part structure with a rectangular chancel and a larger rectangular nave (shortened in 1734); there is a handsome archway between the two.

(BIRSAY, CHRIST CHURCH, Orkney) There were possibly bishops of the Norse diocese of Orkney before 1035. The earliest known seat of the bishopric was at Birsay, though it is uncertain if this was on the mainland or on the tidal island known as the Brough of Birsay. Traces of a twelfth-century building have been found below the present parish church on the mainland, and there are also the lower walls of a twelfth-century church on the Brough, beneath which is the wall of an even earlier building. While there are doubts that the church on the Brough was itself the cathedral, it may have been in some sense a bishop's church both before and after the seat of the bishopric was transferred to Kirkwall in 1137. It has a square chancel with an eastern apse, and a rectangular nave with tusks for a western tower or porch.

BRECHIN, CATHEDRAL OF THE HOLY TRINITY (77 and see 2, 11, 12, and colour plate 1) There was a religious community at Brechin from at least the tenth century and possibly even earlier; several fine carved stones attest to the artistic vigour of this community. There may also have been an early bishop's church, though the first certain reference to a bishop is in about 1150. The first clergy to serve the cathedral were probably the Culdees of the existing community, though Bishop Gregory (1218–42) re-established them as secular canons. Brechin had one of the smallest cathedral chapters, eventually having fourteen canons and seventeen vicars. The diocese itself was small and consisted largely of scattered fragments within the far larger diocese of St Andrews. The cathedral, which has an aisle-less choir, an aisled nave and a north-western tower, was built mainly in the thirteenth century, but incorporates a round tower of Irish type of about 1100 at its south-east corner. Further works in the late fourteenth and early fifteenth centuries included the upper storeys and spire of the north-western tower and the west window. After the Reformation the choir was abandoned and eventually the outer walls of the nave were rebuilt in heightened and simplified form in 1806. The nave was ambitiously restored by John Honeyman in 1900–2, when the clearstorey was re-exposed and a shortened choir was rebuilt. The cathedral remains in use, with the round tower cared for by Historic Scotland.

(CUMBRAE, EPISCOPAL CATHEDRAL OF THE HOLY SPIRIT, Millport, Isle of Cumbrae) The church and associated theological college at Millport on the Isle of Cumbrae were designed for the future sixth Earl of Glasgow by William Butterfield in 1849. They are small-scale masterpieces of High Church Tractarian Gothic. In 1876 the church became the cathedral of the conjoined dioceses of Argyll and the Isles, though its role was diminished when St John at Oban became a cathedral in 1920.

DORNOCH, CATHEDRAL OF ST MARY (78 and see 13–15) Caithness was originally part of the Norse earldom and diocese of Orkney, but a separate Scottish diocese was established by David I. The first record of a bishop occurs between 1147 and 1151; his main church seems to have been at Halkirk in Caithness. The cathedral was fixed at Dornoch (in what came to be Sutherland) in the time of Bishop (Saint) Gilbert de Moravia (1222–45); he also established a chapter of ten secular canons, which was eventually increased to thirteen. Gilbert built a cathedral church, with rectangular choir and transepts of approximately equal size; it eventually had an aisled nave, though it is not certain if this was a primary feature. After the Reformation the cathedral was devastated during a feud in 1570 and was left roofless until the choir and transepts were repaired in 1614–22. Restoration by Alexander Coupar in 1835–7 placed plaster vaults over the eastern parts and reconstructed the nave as an aisle-less rectangle. A later restoration in 1924–7 stripped Coupar's lath-and-plaster strapping off the walls, but left his plaster vaults. It remains in use.

DUNBLANE, CATHEDRAL OF ST BLANE (**79** and see **4, 28–33, 57, 70** and **colour plate 6**) The survival of cross slabs suggests there was a community here by the eighth or the ninth century, though there is also a tradition that links the site with St Blane in the late sixth or the early seventh century. The first recorded bishop is Laurence, in 1155. Initially there may have been two cathedral centres: one at Dunblane in Menteith, and the other at Muthill in Strathearn, and there are architecturally related mid-twelfth-century towers at the two places. After a period of decline, the diocese was revived by Bishop Clement (1233–58), a Dominican friar, who considered moving the seat of the bishopric to the Augustinian abbey of Inchaffray. Once he had decided on Dunblane he started to form a chapter which included initially the monastic heads of the area, but was composed eventually of secular canons. The eventual number of canons was sixteen, with twelve chaplains. Clement also started to build a new cathedral church, with an elongated rectangular choir flanked by a two-storeyed chapter house and sacristy range along its north flank and an eight-bay aisled nave. The design of the nave, which absorbed the twelfth-century tower in its south aisle, seems to have been modified on at least two occasions during construction; the choir was probably the last part to be completed, towards the end of the century. The final identifiable structural changes took place under the three Chisholm bishops, who ruled the diocese between 1487 and 1569; they heightened the tower, rebuilt the choir parapet and formed a new chapel within the west end of the north nave aisle. One of them also provided canopied choir stalls, of which a number survive. The nave was abandoned after the Reformation. The choir, which was taken over by the parish, underwent major restoration by James Gillespie Graham in 1816–19, and there was further work by Sir George Gilbert Scott in 1873. But the main campaign of restoration was directed by Sir Robert Rowand Anderson in 1889–93, which brought the nave back into use. Additional furnishings were designed by Sir Robert Lorimer in 1911–12. Although still in use the cathedral is cared for by Historic Scotland.

DUNDEE, EPISCOPAL CATHEDRAL OF ST PAUL The church was begun for Bishop Alexander Penrose Forbes to the designs of Sir George Gilbert Scott in 1853, and became the cathedral of Brechin diocese in 1904. It has an apsidal choir, transepts and an aisled nave; the greatest architectural emphasis is provided by the soaring west tower and spire. The telescoped main body of the tower is based on that of the nearby medieval parish church, but it is capped by a spire rather than the crown steeple originally planned for its prototype.

DUNDEE, ROMAN CATHOLIC CATHEDRAL OF ST ANDREW The church was built as a rectangular hall church by George Mathewson in 1835–6, in simplified English perpendicular style, and the apse for the high altar was part of a remodelling by C.J. Menart in 1921. The church was designated pro-cathedral of the dioceses of Dunkeld, Dunblane and Brechin in 1886, and became a full cathedral in 1923.

DUNKELD, CATHEDRAL OF ST COLUMBA (**80**, and see **35, 47, 48, 56, 58, 59**) Dunkeld may have been briefly the main centre of the Scottish church in the mid-ninth century, when King Kenneth macAlpin transferred some of the relics of St Columba there from Iona in 849, and in 869 the abbot of the community was described as the chief bishop of the kingdom. A number of early carved stones survive from around this period. The first bishop of the revived diocese appears on record in about 1114, and he seems to have been supported at first by the clergy of the diocese, though a chapter of secular canons began to develop from the early thirteenth century. There were eventually twenty-two canons and thirteen vicars. The building history of the cathedral is partly recorded by Abbot Alexander Myln of Cambuskenneth in his account of the lives of the bishops: Myln had earlier been dean of part of the diocese. The oldest part of the building is the mid-thirteenth-century choir. The nave was started by Bishop Robert Cardeny in 1406 and was completed by Bishop Thomas Lauder (1452–75), who went on to add a south nave porch and to build a square chapter house and sacristy to the north of the choir in 1457. Lauder also started the north-west tower in 1469, which was completed by Bishop James Livingstone (1475–83). Many fine furnishings were provided, particularly by Lauder and by Bishop George Brown (1483–1515). The cathedral was 'cleansed' on 12 August 1560, and the roof of the nave was removed soon after, probably after the parishioners had started to use the choir as their church. There were major restorations by Archibald Elliot in 1814–15 and by Dunn and Watson in 1908. The choir remains in use, with the rest cared for by Historic Scotland.

EDINBURGH, CATHEDRAL OF ST GILES (**81** and see **66**) The parish church of Edinburgh, which became one of the finest of the great medieval burgh churches, was elevated to cathedral status by Charles I in 1633. There was a church here from the twelfth century, but the core of the building, as now seen, was probably a cross-shaped aisled building of the later fourteenth century. This core was almost entirely subsumed within a series of additions made in the course of the later fourteenth, fifteenth and sixteenth centuries, which both heightened parts of the original building and added large numbers of chapels around its perimeter. The church was made collegiate in 1468–9. Together, all of the additions resulted in an attractive though extremely irregular external appearance, but this was eventually reduced to a more symmetrical appearance in a draconian restoration by William Burn in 1829–33. Virtually the only feature now externally identifiable as medieval is the central tower with its crown steeple, though much original work survives internally. The church remains in use.

EDINBURGH, EPISCOPAL CATHEDRAL OF ST MARY

This is the most architecturally ambitious of the post-Reformation cathedrals. It was built between 1874 and 1917 to the designs of Sir George Gilbert Scott and his sons John Oldrid and Charles Oldrid, with money left for this purpose by Mary and Barbara Walker. It is a cruciform building with aisles to all parts, and with stone vaults over the choir and aisles, but with a timber wagon ceiling over the nave. North of the choir is a square chapter house with an octagonal superstructure. The most notable feature is the magnificent triplet of spires which together provide one of the city's finest landmarks.

EDINBURGH, ROMAN CATHOLIC CATHEDRAL OF ST MARY

This was built as a spacious hall church to the design of James Gillespie Graham in 1813, in a version of the English perpendicular style. Since it was made the cathedral of the archdiocese in 1878 it has been extensively rebuilt, leaving the façade as the only survivor of the original church. In 1891, after a fire, John Biggar added nave aisles and a clearstorey; in 1895 Buchanan and Bennett built the aisled and apsed choir; in 1932 Reid and Forbes raised the nave and provided a new roof; and a new porch was built by T. Harley Haddow in 1976–7.

ELGIN, CATHEDRAL OF THE HOLY TRINITY

(82, and see 1, 16–18, 40, 41, 52, 62, 64, 67 and colour plates 3 and 7) Bishops may have been appointed in the province of Moray by the mormaers (local rulers) from the eleventh century, but the first bishop whose name we know was Giric or Gregory, who is on record in about 1114. After the area came under centralized control around the 1130s bishops began to be appointed more regularly from the 1150s onwards. The earlier bishops had moved around between churches at Birnie, Kineddar and Spynie, until they fixed first on Spynie as their cathedral in 1207–8 and then on Elgin in 1224. By the time of the move to Elgin, the diocese already had a chapter of secular canons with a constitution based on that of Lincoln. There were eventually twenty-five canons, eighteen vicars and varying numbers of chaplains. Construction of the cathedral at Elgin was started at about the time of the move of 1224; it was initially given an aisle-less choir and transepts, an aisled nave and three towers, though the two west towers may have been an afterthought. After a fire in 1270 the choir was extended, with aisles added along much of its length, and an octagonal chapter house was built north of the choir; outer aisles were added along the nave flanks (incorporating an earlier chapel on the

south aisle), with a south porch. Further extensive rebuilding and repair was necessitated by a fire in 1390. The cathedral was abandoned soon after the Reformation in favour of the nearby parish church, and the lead of the roofs was removed in 1568; the collapse of the central tower in 1711 left the building a strikingly beautiful ruin. It is cared for by Historic Scotland.

FORTROSE, CATHEDRAL OF SS PETER AND BONIFACE

(83 and see 34, 50, 51 and colour plate 8) It has been suggested there was a diocese in Ross, centred on Rosemarkie, as early as around 700, and it has also been argued that St Duthac was a bishop there in the mid-eleventh century. However, the first certainly recorded bishop was Macbeth, in the years around 1130. A chapter of canons begins to appear in the thirteenth century, and there were eventually twenty-one canons and about five vicars. It is not known when the cathedral was first moved to Fortrose, but the building seems initially to have been basically an extended rectangle, from which projected a north-western tower and a two-storeyed rectangular chapter house and sacristy block on the north side of the choir. The latter is of the thirteenth century. There may also have been a south nave aisle but, if so, it was later incorporated within an elegant but small-scale aisle and chapel of the late fourteenth century, which are traditionally attributed to Euphemia Countess of Ross. The only upstanding parts of the building are the sacristy and chapter house range and the south nave aisle and chapel, which are maintained by Historic Scotland.

GLASGOW, CATHEDRAL OF ST KENTIGERN (OR MUNGO)

(84, 85 and see 19–27, 46, 53, 54, 63 and colour plates 2, 5) It is thought the first bishop to serve this area was St Kentigern, who died in 612, and who is said to have built his church in a cemetery earlier consecrated by St Ninian. After Kentigern the first named bishop of the diocese is recorded around 1060, though it is not until the time of Bishop John (c. 1114–47) that true diocesan bishops begin to appear. John started to assemble a chapter of secular canons, which eventually numbered thirty-two (the largest complement in Scotland), with many vicars and chaplains. Glasgow became Scotland's second archbishopric in 1492. Bishop John started to build a cathedral, which was ready for dedication in 1136, and this was enlarged by Bishop Jocelin, with a second dedication in 1197. Recent excavations have shown the structures raised at those times were more complex than previously supposed, and a fragment of the latter survives in the crypt. However, the cathedral now seen is mainly of the thirteenth century. The lower walls of the transepts and nave were started in the early years of the century, but the main effort moved back to the eastern limb following a decision of about 1240 to construct an enlarged choir in the time of Bishop William Bondington. The choir was a rectangle of five aisled bays with an eastern ambulatory and chapels beyond, and with two-storeyed blocks on its north side for chapter houses, sacristy and treasury. The choir was elevated above a crypt of extraordinary spatial subtlety. The transepts projected no further than the line of the aisles, though a start was also made on a massive single asymmetrical projection off the south transept, of which only the crypt was completed. The nave, which was largely finished towards the end of the century, was of eight aisled bays, its plan being partly conditioned by the earlier lower walls. It eventually had two western towers, neither of which was part of the original scheme. Repairs after a fire in about 1400 resulted in a new central tower and spire and a rebuilt upper chapter house. After the Reformation the cathedral was progressively subdivided to house three congregations (two of which were removed in 1798 and 1835); the only major structural losses have been the two western towers, demolished in the 1840s. Although still in use it is cared for by Historic Scotland.

GLASGOW, EPISCOPAL CATHEDRAL OF ST MARY The church was built in a thirteenth-century English style to the designs of Sir George Gilbert Scott in 1871–8, with the spire on the tower in the junction between the south transept and choir being completed to the designs of John Oldrid Scott in 1893. It became a cathedral in 1907.

GLASGOW, GREEK ORTHODOX CATHEDRAL OF ST LUKE This was built in 1876–7, as Bellhaven Church, for a United Presbyterian congregation. It was designed in an early-thirteenth-century English style by James Sellars. It became a cathedral in 1954.

GLASGOW, ROMAN CATHOLIC CATHEDRAL OF ST ANDREW (see 73) This was started in 1814 on the bank of the Clyde as a large chapel in the fourteenth-century English style; the architect was James Gillespie Graham. The nave is of six aisled bays with an eastern apse for the high altar, the whole being covered by plaster vaults. There were originally galleries in the aisles. It became the cathedral of the archdiocese in 1889.

(HODDOM, Dumfries-shire) St Kentigern of Glasgow is said to have based his episcopal activities here for a while in the late sixth century. Several important early carved stones have been found in the vicinity, and excavations in 1991–2 located traces of what could be a Northumbrian monastery.

INVERNESS, EPISCOPAL CATHEDRAL OF ST ANDREW (see 72) The cathedral in Inverness was built to serve the bishops of the dioceses of Moray, Ross and Caithness. It was started in 1866 to the designs of Alexander Ross. The five-bay aisled nave terminates in a west front emphasized by a pair of towers for which spires were originally planned; the

nave is separated by transepts from the aisled choir, which has an eastern apse.

IONA, CATHEDRAL OF ST MARY (86 and see 65 and colour plate 12) There may have been bishops associated with the community established here by Columba in 565, and there are certainly references to bishops between the seventh and mid-tenth centuries. There were plans to make the Benedictine abbey of Iona the cathedral church of the Scottish part of the diocese of the Isles in 1498, though nothing seems to have come of this, and it was only after the Reformation that it was regarded as a cathedral. A chapter of some sort was constituted in 1617, though it was probably in the 1630s, in the time of Charles I, that the eastern parts of the abbey church were adapted to fit them for brief use as a cathedral. The abbey itself had been founded in about 1200, from which period the north transept survives, but the church was extensively rebuilt in the course of the thirteenth and fifteenth centuries, resulting ultimately in a cruciform structure with an aisle-less nave and a choir flanked by a south aisle and a northern sacristy. After falling into ruin the church and monastic buildings have been progressively restored in an operation started in the 1870s for the Duke of Argyll, and they now serve the Iona Community.

(KINGARTH, St Blane, Bute) Kingarth is traditionally associated with the episcopate of St Blane in the later sixth century. The *Annals of Ulster* record the deaths of bishops here in the later seventh century and of abbots in the eighth century. Remains of an early monastery may be represented by a 'bean-shaped' enclosure and what could be traces of cells. The most substantial remains now on the site are of the shell of the two-part parish church of St Blane, dating from the mid-twelfth century, the east end of which was rebuilt in the thirteenth century; it is in the care of Historic Scotland.

(KINNEDDAR, see Spynie)

(KINRIMUND, KILRIMONT, see St Andrews)

KIRKWALL, CATHEDRAL OF ST MAGNUS (87 and see 8, 36–38, 60, 69 and colour plate 4) There may have been bishops of Orkney before 1035, and a cathedral for them was built at Birsay some time between 1048 and 1065. The earlier bishops were subject variously to York, Hamburg-Bremen and Lund until 1153, when they became subject to Trondheim. By then the decision had been taken to transfer the seat of the diocese from Birsay to Kirkwall in 1137. A chapter of secular canons was beginning to take shape by the mid-thirteenth century, and there were eventually fifteen canons and thirteen chaplains. After the Northern Isles had been pledged by Norway to Scotland the diocese was placed under the authority of the new archdiocese of St Andrews in 1472. The cathedral started at

Kirkwall in about 1137 was set out on a grand scale, to a cruciform plan with a central tower; it eventually had vaulting over all parts. The eastern limb was initially of two and a half bays terminating in apses, while the nave was of eight bays. In the process of building there were several expansions on the original plan: most notably, the eastern limb was extended by three bays, while a triple portal was built at the west front. But construction of the later parts was painfully slow, and they were only eventually roofed on the eve of the Reformation; indeed the vaulting over the west bays of the nave was completed in the 1970s – in fibreglass.

LISMORE, CATHEDRAL OF ST MOLUOC (88 and see 42) The diocese of Argyll was carved out of that of Dunkeld at some date between 1183 and 1188. It may have been centred on the island of Lismore from the start, and was certainly there from 1225, though there were thoughts of moving it to a more convenient place in 1249. The site can never have been very suitable, and in 1512 it was suggested the defunct Cistercian abbey of Saddell should become the cathedral, though this was not acted upon. A chapter of secular canons only began to appear in the second half of the fourteenth century, and there may eventually have been as many as twelve canons. The cathedral was a simple aisle-less buttressed rectangle, possibly of early fourteenth-century date, with no structural distinction between nave and choir. There was a small western tower and perhaps a simple sacristy and chapter house north of the choir. The nave and tower, of which virtually nothing remains, were probably abandoned soon after the Reformation, and the whole building was roofless by 1679; the choir, which was brought back into use, was restored in 1749 and again in about 1900 and 1956.

(MORTLACH, St Moluoc, Banffshire) Up to the earlier 1130s the bishops of Aberdeen are said to have been based at Mortlach, where the survival of an early cross slab points to a long Christian history. The present church incorporates its medieval predecessor, and has a grouping of narrow lancets in its east wall; it now has the overall appearance of a thirteenth-century building that was much adapted in the nineteenth century.

MOTHERWELL, ROMAN CATHOLIC CATHEDRAL OF OUR LADY OF GOOD AID The church was built in 1900–1 to the designs of Peter Paul Pugin at a cost of nearly £8000. It is a basilica with an eastern apse, in the English decorated style. It became the cathedral of the new diocese of Motherwell in 1948.

(MUTHILL, Perthshire) (see 6) Some of the earlier bishops of the diocese that was eventually permanently based on Dunblane seem to have preferred the Strathearn part of their diocese. They may have used a church at Muthill in Strathearn as their cathedral, where there was a community of Culdees by the late twelfth century if not earlier. Since the mid-twelfth-century tower of the church shows significant similarities with the larger tower at Dunblane, it is possible both were built around the same time, perhaps suggesting they were regarded as twin cathedral centres. In the course of the Middle Ages the church progressively acquired an aisled nave and aisle-less chancel, at least part of which is traditionally ascribed to Michael Ochiltree when dean of Dunblane (c. 1419–29). It was abandoned after a new church was built in 1826–8, and its shell is now cared for by Historic Scotland.

OBAN, EPISCOPAL CATHEDRAL OF ST JOHN THE DIVINE The first Episcopal church on this site was built in 1864 by J. Thomson, and it was extended in 1882. The foundations of a new building designed by James Chalmers were laid in 1910, and its eastern parts were built to the east of the original building. This incomplete building was made the cathedral of the conjoined dioceses of Argyll and the Isles in 1920. A completely new building was designed by Harold Tarbolton in 1928 and yet another by Ian Lindsay in 1958, but nothing was done in either case apart from the insertion of a screen by Ian Lindsay. The cathedral remains an intriguingly ungainly product of the campaigns of 1864, 1882 and 1910.

OBAN, ROMAN CATHOLIC CATHEDRAL OF ST COLUMBA A wooden pro-cathedral was built for Lord Bute in 1886. The foundation stone of the new cathedral, designed by Sir Giles Gilbert Scott, was laid in 1932, and it was built between 1935 and 1952. It is an imposingly austere Gothic aisled structure with a western tower, constructed of granite.

PAISLEY, ROMAN CATHOLIC CATHEDRAL OF ST MIRIN The church was built in 1930–2 in a Romanesque style by Thomas Baird. It became the cathedral of the new diocese in 1948.

PERTH, EPISCOPAL CATHEDRAL OF ST NINIAN (see 71) Perth's was the first cathedral to be started in Scotland since the Reformation, though there was controversy within the church over the project, which owed much to the enthusiasm of Lord Forbes and the future Earl of Glasgow. It was built for the united dioceses of St Andrews, Dunkeld and Dunblane, and was designed in 1849 in the English decorated style by William Butterfield. The eastern parts were completed by 1850 and the nave in 1888–90. There were major alterations in 1901–11 by J.L. and F.L. Pearson, which included the replacement of the incomplete west tower by a new west front, and the construction of an apsidal Lady chapel to the south of the chancel.

ST ANDREWS, CATHEDRAL OF ST ANDREW
(**89** and see **3, 9, 10, 39, 45** and **colour plate 10**)
According to one tradition, the history of Kinrimund
or Kilrimont goes back to the fourth century, though
the earliest reference to a religious community here is
to the death of its abbot in 747. It is possible that
relics of St Andrew were brought here by the exiled
Bishop Acca of Hexham in about 732. By the mid-
ninth century Kilrimont had become the chief centre
of the Scottish church, a position it retained
throughout the Middle Ages. References to bishops of
the Scots here begin in about the tenth century, which
suggests they were regarded as chief bishops (though
it was not until 1472 that St Andrews became the
country's first archbishopric). A variety of
communities was superseded by Augustinian canons
in 1144, who acted as the cathedral chapter until the
Reformation. The earliest surviving building thought
to have served as a cathedral is the church now called
St Rule's, to the south-east of the later cathedral. It
was probably first built as a three-cell structure, but
was later extended to both east and west. The date of
this building is hotly debated, with many advocating
a late eleventh-century date for the earlier part,
though on balance it appears more likely to date from
two operations in the first half of the twelfth century.
A new cathedral was set out by Bishop Arnold soon
after 1160 to an extended cruciform plan, with an
aisle-less presbytery, a choir of six aisled bays and a
nave probably intended to be of fourteen (but
eventually of only twelve) aisled bays. It was by far
the largest cathedral in Scotland. After delays caused
by the collapse of the incomplete west front in the
1270s and the outbreak of the Wars of Independence,
it was eventually dedicated in 1318. A fire in 1378
and the collapse of the south transept gable in 1409
necessitated further major rebuilding. The cathedral
was 'cleansed' on the eve of the Reformation
following a sermon by John Knox on 11 June 1559,
and was soon abandoned in favour of the parish
church. Its remains are now cared for by Historic
Scotland.

SNIZORT (Skye) The earlier bishops of the Norse
diocese which embraced both the Isle of Man and the
Scottish Isles (known variously as the diocese of the
Isles, of Man, Skye, Sodor or Sudreys) were subject
first to York and later to Trondheim. There was a
cathedral at Peel on Man by 1231, but from 1387 the
Scottish part of the diocese began to develop
separately, based on what may have been an earlier
episcopal centre on the island of Skeabost in the River
Snizort on Skye. Snizort was evidently never a
satisfactory base for the diocese, and it is doubtful
how far there was ever a chapter of canons; there
were pleas to remove it elsewhere in 1433 and again
in 1498 (to Iona). There are the remains of a number
of simple rectangular chapels on the island, though
how any of these may have served as a cathedral is
difficult to say.

(SPYNIE, HOLY TRINITY, Moray) (**61** and see
colour plate 11) Spynie was one of the earlier bases of
the diocese of Moray, and became additionally
important after the decision was taken to fix the
cathedral there in 1207–8 and before it was moved to
Elgin in 1224. The church used as a cathedral may
have survived in modified form as the parish church
until a new building was constructed elsewhere in
1736. Its foundations were said to be visible until as
recently as 1924, and the east end of the church is
now marked by a re-erected cross, while the position
of its west front is recorded on a burial enclosure.
The bishops continued to have a major fortified
residence at Spynie throughout the Middle Ages and
beyond, the imposing remains of which are now
cared for by Historic Scotland. (Traces of a church in
the graveyard, and of the bishop's residence to its
north, were also said to be visible in the late
nineteenth century at Kinneddar, another of the early
episcopal centres of the diocese of Moray.)

**WHITHORN, CATHEDRAL OF ST MARTIN OF
TOURS** (**90** and see **5, 68** and **colour plate 9**)
Whithorn is associated with the fifth-century
episcopal mission of St Ninian to an existing
Christian community; after a lapse of four centuries
there are references to several further bishops in the
eighth century, though the site by then had become
essentially monastic. Recent excavations down the
hill from the cathedral have cast much light on the
life of the Northumbrian monastery, and there is an
important collection of carved stones in the site
museum, the earliest of which could date from the
fifth century. The first known bishop of a revived
diocese of Galloway is referred to in 1128, but until
the mid-fourteenth century the diocese was subject to
York. A priory of Augustinian canons may have acted
as the first cathedral chapter, as at St Andrews,
though by 1177 there was a community of the stricter
order of Premonstratensian canons. The chief
structural remains of the cathedral are of the aisle-less
nave, which was adapted to serve as a post-
Reformation parish church. The plan of the eastern
limb and transepts have been partly revealed by
excavation; however, it is unclear whether the
unaisled eastern extremity, which was carried on a
reconstructed crypt, was a low chapel beyond an
ambulatory or a full-height presbytery. The functions
of other parts are also unclear, though the projection
at the north-east corner may have been a sacristy and
treasury. The cathedral appears to have been
completely unroofed after the Reformation, but the
nave was reroofed in the early seventeenth century for
parochial use, though the collapse of its western
tower in 1684 led to its truncation by one bay. It
continued to serve as a parish church until a new one
was built over the east claustral range of the priory in
1822. The site of the cathedral is maintained by
Historic Scotland.

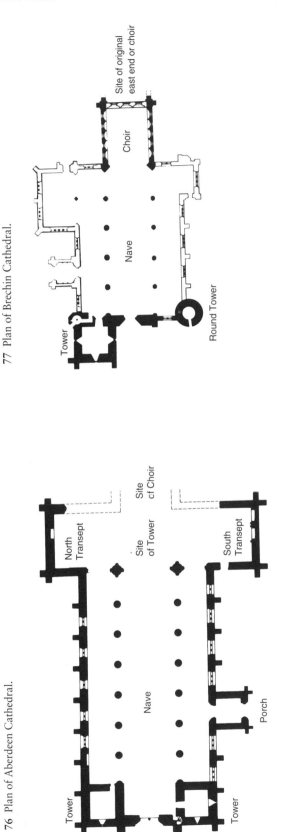

76 Plan of Aberdeen Cathedral.

77 Plan of Brechin Cathedral.

78 Plan of Dornoch Cathedral.

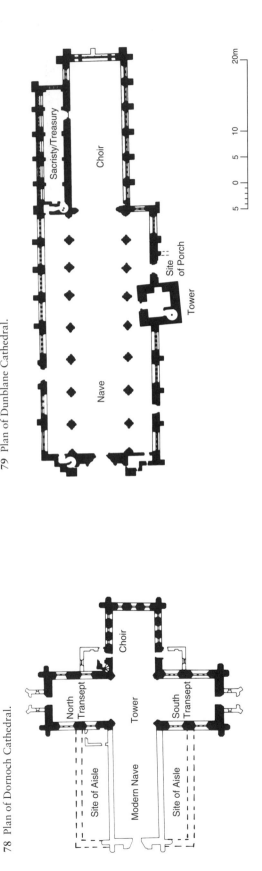

79 Plan of Dunblane Cathedral.

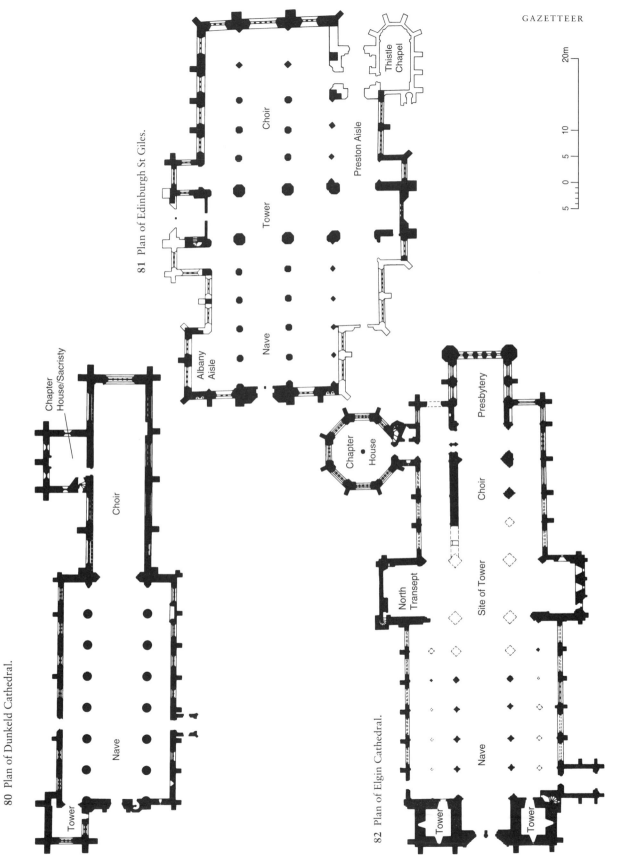

80 Plan of Dunkeld Cathedral.

81 Plan of Edinburgh St Giles.

82 Plan of Elgin Cathedral.

83 Plan of Fortrose Cathedral.

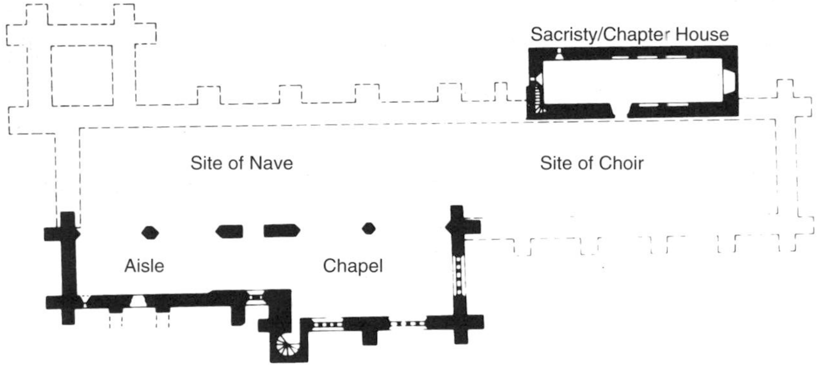

Site of Tower

Sacristy/Chapter House

Site of Nave

Site of Choir

Chapel

Aisle

84 Plan of Glasgow Cathedral at the main level.

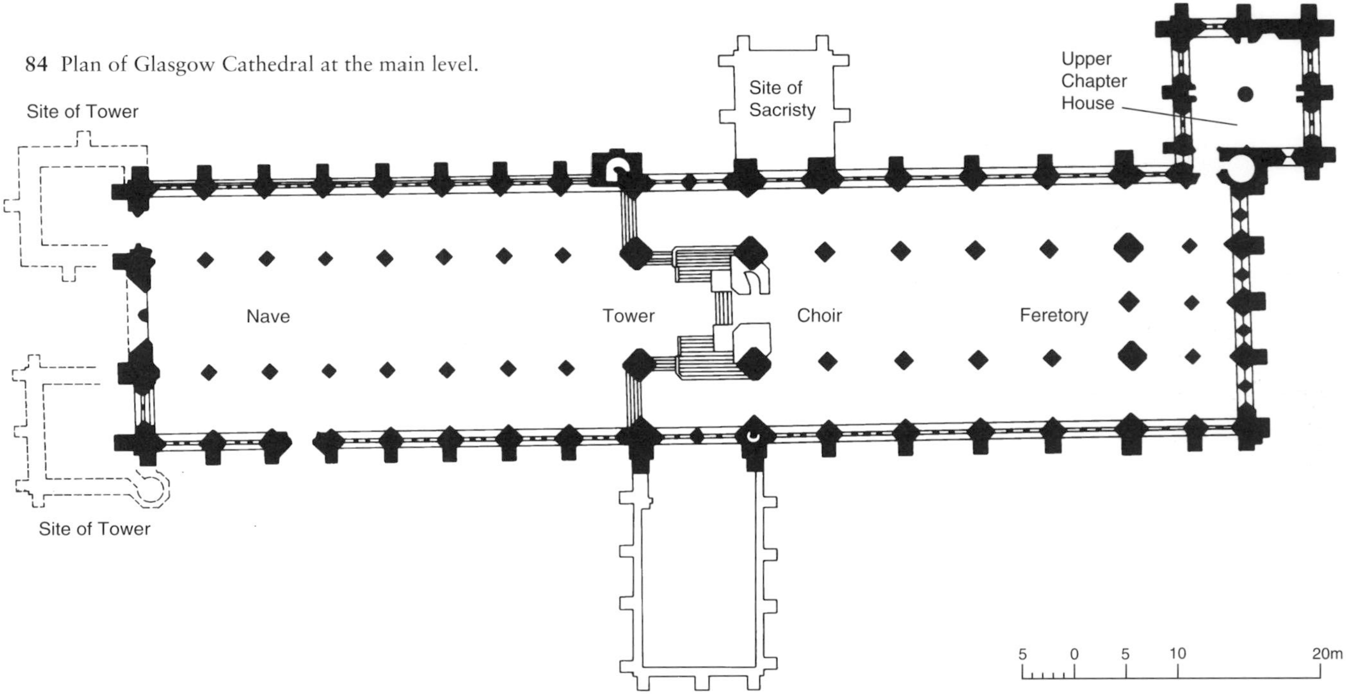

Upper Chapter House

Site of Sacristy

Feretory

Choir

Tower

Nave

Site of Tower

Site of Tower

20m

10

5

0

5

5

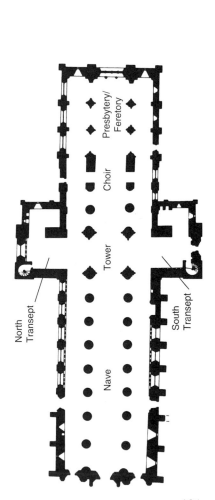

85 Plan of Glasgow Cathedral at the crypt level.

86 Plan of Iona Abbey.

87 Plan of Kirkwall Cathedral.

88 Plan of Lismore Cathedral.

Plan of Glasgow Cathedral at the crypt level:
Lower Chapter House
Treasury
Site of Tomb
Lady Chapel
Blackadder Aisle

Plan of Iona Abbey:
Sacristy
Choir
North Transept
Tower
South Transept
Nave
Site of Thirteenth-Century Aisle

Plan of Kirkwall Cathedral:
Presbytery/Feretory
Choir
Tower
North Transept
South Transept
Nave

Plan of Lismore Cathedral:
Site of Sacristy
Choir
Site of Nave
Site of Tower
20m

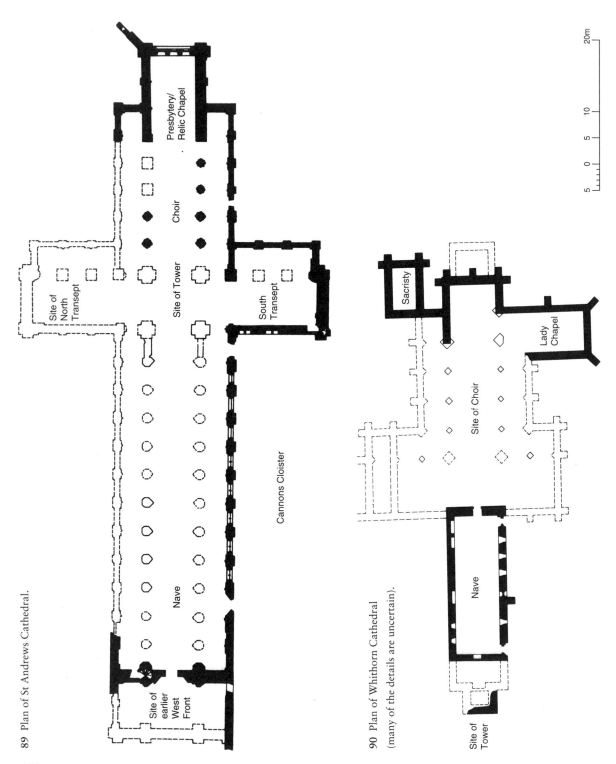

89 Plan of St Andrews Cathedral.

Presbytery/Relic Chapel

Choir

Site of North Transept

Site of Tower

South Transept

Cannons Cloister

Nave

Site of earlier West Front

90 Plan of Whithorn Cathedral (many of the details are uncertain).

Sacristy

Lady Chapel

Site of Choir

Nave

Site of Tower

20m

Further reading

Guidebooks are available at most of the cathedrals of medieval foundation and also at many of those of more recent construction. Descriptions of some of the cathedrals can be found in the Inventories of the Royal Commission on the Ancient and Historical Monuments of Scotland, in the Buildings of Scotland series, and in the illustrated architectural guides of the Royal Incorporation of Architects in Scotland. Discussions of various aspects of cathedral history are covered in a growing number of excellent publications by the Societies of Friends of several cathedrals. The historical background to the building of the cathedrals is well covered in the relevant volumes of The Edinburgh History of Scotland (volumes by A.A.M. Duncan, Ranald Nicholson and Gordon Donaldson), The New History of Scotland (volumes by Alfred P. Smyth, G.W.S. Barrow, Alexander Grant and Jenny Wormald) and Michael Lynch's *Scotland, a new history*. Apart from those, the following highly selective list of books and articles can be recommended (many of which contain guidance on further reading).

General church history

Barrow, G.W.S., The *kingdom of the Scots*, London, 1973.

Burleigh, J.H.S., *A church history of Scotland*, Oxford, 1960.

Cockburn, James Hutchison, *The medieval bishops of Dunblane and their church*, Edinburgh, 1959.

Cowan, Ian B. and Easson, David, *Medieval religious houses, Scotland*, 2nd edn, London, 1976.

Donaldson, Gordon, *Scottish church history*, Edinburgh, 1985.

Dowden, John, *The medieval church in Scotland*, Glasgow, 1910.

Macfarlane, Leslie J., *William Elphinstone and the kingdom of Scotland*, Aberdeen, 1985.

Watt, D.E.R., *Fasti ecclesiae Scoticanae medii aevi*, 2nd edn, Scottish Record Society, Edinburgh, 1969 (lists of the bishops and senior clergy of the cathedrals).

The architecture of the cathedrals and its background

Crawford, Barbara (ed.), *St Magnus cathedral and Orkney's twelfth-century renaissance*, Aberdeen, 1988.

Cruden, Stewart, *Scottish medieval churches*, Edinburgh, 1986.

Eyre-Todd, George (ed.), *The book of Glasgow Cathedral*, Glasgow, 1898.

Fawcett, Richard, *Scottish architecture from the accession of the Stewarts to the Reformation, 1371–1560*, Edinburgh, 1994.

Lindsay, Ian Gordon, *The cathedrals of Scotland*, Edinburgh, 1926.

MacGibbon, David and Ross, Thomas, *The ecclesiastical architecture of Scotland*, 3 vols., Edinburgh, 1896–7.

McRoberts, David (ed.), *The medieval church of St Andrews*, Glasgow, 1976.

The life and worship of the cathedrals

Cowan, Ian B., *The medieval church in Scotland*, Edinburgh, 1995.

Cowan, Ian B., *St Machar's Cathedral in the early middle ages*, Friends of St Machar's Cathedral, occasional papers no. 6, 1980.

Donaldson, Gordon, *The faith of the Scots*, London, 1990.

Dowden, John, *The bishops of Scotland*, Glasgow, 1912.

Dunlop, Annie, 'Life in a medieval cathedral', *Society of Friends of Dunblane Cathedral*, vol. 4, 1945.

Durkan, John, 'Notes on Glasgow Cathedral, the medieval altars', *Innes Review*, vol. 21, 1970.

Durkan, John, *The precinct of Glasgow Cathedral*, Society of Friends of Glasgow Cathedral, 1986.

Forrester, Duncan and Murray, Douglas, (eds.) *Studies in the history of worship in Scotland*, Edinburgh, 1984.

McRoberts, David, 'The medieval Scottish liturgy illustrated by surviving documents', *Transactions of the Scottish Ecclesiological Society*, vol. 15, 1957.

McRoberts, David, 'The manse of Stobo in 1542', *Innes Review*, vol. 22, 1971.

The cathedrals since the Reformation

Anson, Peter F., *The Catholic Church in modern Scotland*, London, 1937.

Anson, Peter F., 'Catholic church building in Scotland from the Reformation until the outbreak of the First World War', *Innes Review*, vol. 5, 1954.

Cowan, Ian B., *The Scottish Reformation*, London, 1982.

Goldie, Frederick, *A short history of the Episcopal Church in Scotland*, 2nd ed, Edinburgh, 1976.

Hay, George, *The architecture of Scottish post-Reformation churches*, Oxford, 1957.

Lochhead, Marion, *Episcopal Scotland in the nineteenth century*, London, 1966.

McRoberts, David, 'Material destruction caused by the Scottish Reformation', *Innes Review*, vol. 10, 1959.

Index

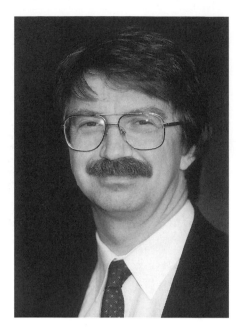

The author
Dr Richard Fawcett is a Principal Inspector of
Ancient Monuments with Historic Scotland. He
is an architectural historian with particular
interest in medieval churches and has published a
number of articles and guidebooks.